Anointed
But
Illegal!

PETER A HAMILTON

Foreword by Pastor David Camp, Jr.

WESTBOW
P R E S S®
A DIVISION OF THOMAS NELSON
& ZONDERVAN

This book is a work of non-fiction. Unless otherwise noted, the author and the publisher make no explicit guarantees as to the accuracy of the information contained in this book and in some cases, names of people and places have been altered to protect their privacy.

WestBow Press books may be ordered through booksellers or by contacting:

WestBow Press
A Division of Thomas Nelson & Zondervan
1663 Liberty Drive
Bloomington, IN 47403
www.westbowpress.com
844-714-3454

Because of the dynamic nature of the Internet, any web addresses or links contained in this book may have changed since publication and may no longer be valid. The views expressed in this work are solely those of the author and do not necessarily reflect the views of the publisher, and the publisher hereby disclaims any responsibility for them.

Any people depicted in stock imagery provided by Getty Images are models, and such images are being used for illustrative purposes only.
Certain stock imagery © Getty Images.

Scripture quotations marked NKJV are taken from the New King James Version. Copyright © 1982 by Thomas Nelson, Inc. Used by permission. All rights reserved.

Scripture quotations marked AMP are taken from the Amplified® Bible, Copyright © 1954, 1958, 1962, 1964, 1965, 1987 by The Lockman Foundation. Used by permission.

Scripture quotations marked NLT are taken from the Holy Bible, New Living Translation, copyright © 1996, 2004, 2007 by Tyndale House Foundation. Used by permission of Tyndale House Publishers, Inc., Carol Stream, Illinois 60188. All rights reserved.

ISBN: 979-8-3850-1768-3 (sc)
ISBN: 979-8-3850-1769-0 (hc)
ISBN: 979-8-3850-1770-6 (e)

Library of Congress Control Number: 2024901767

Print information available on the last page.

WestBow Press rev. date: 03/04/2024

Blessed be the LORD,
the God of

_____

May the grace of God locate you at the time of your
need. May His goodness and mercy pursue you daily, as
you purpose in your heart to walk with God from this
moment onward. Receive it in Jesus's name. Amen.

Date: _____

Signature: _____

Pastor Peter A Hamilton

I dedicate this book first to my Heavenly Father. I thank Him for the ability and gift, for calling me to teach His people the truth of His word, and for entrusting me with His work in the United States of America.

CONTENTS

FOREWORD

PASTOR DAVID CAMP, JR.

This is a much needed book on what it means to be *a true anointed servant* of God. This foreword is written by Pastor David Camp, Jr., the founder and pastor of the Agape Apostolic Church in Troy, New York. It is with sincere appreciation and great admiration that I acknowledge Pastor Peter A. Hamilton, whom I find to be a true man of God with impeccable integrity.

Pastor Peter loves God and the people of God. His love for God and the upbuilding of the ministry is the catalyst behind this powerful book on what it means to be a true anointed servant of God. I thank Pastor Peter A. Hamilton for acknowledging the Lord through prayer and consecrated fasting to be led by the Lord to write this much needed instructional manual on being *anointed but illegal*. Pastor Peter's purpose in writing this book is to set in order the declaration for what it means to be *anointed men and women* for the upbuilding of the kingdom of God.

It is germane that every man and woman who is called by God into ministry fully comprehend what it means to be *anointed but illegal*. The importance of being *truly anointed by the Lord* cannot be overemphasized or understated. Isaiah wrote about *the importance of the anointing* in Isaiah 10:27. Luke wrote about *the importance of the anointing* in Luke 4:18–19. John wrote about *the importance of the anointing* in 1 John 2:27. May the Lord Jesus Christ enlarge the ministry of every individual who prayerfully and sincerely receives and meditates on the teaching from this book on being *anointed but illegal*. The ministry thanks you, Pastor Peter A. Hamilton.

PREFACE

I put pen to paper to bring some understanding of our community and the nation in which we live. First, you must recognize the downfall of your community. This will allow you to figure out what steps you can take toward recovery and how to bring changes to your community so it can be a better place to live.

Your children, your grandchildren, and your entire lineage should be able to live a decent and moral life in accordance with God's Word. You and the *legacy* you leave behind will lay this foundation. Legacy can be *truth or lies*; it depends upon the choices you are willing to make.

This temporary abode that we call home can be a better place before you die, if you decide to make the right choices and do everything in your power to bring about changes and reformation. These must occur first in your home, your community, and in your nation. Every one of us has been born into a different family background and a multitude of different religious beliefs, culture, and traditions. This book will enlighten you, the reader, and help you make the right decision in leaving a *legacy of truth* for the betterment of your family lineage, community, and nation.

Have you ever asked yourself where all these different religions, culture, traditions, and millions of gods came from? When did they come into existence? Is the *Father of Spirits* responsible for it? *No! He's not responsible.*

Jesus Christ came not only to bring correction to these things. He came to deliver His *covenant* people out of it and to give Himself as the ultimate sacrifice. He could then reconcile humankind with the Father.

Jesus's opposition was the religious leaders of His time. He neither introduced nor brought another religion because religion can't help anyone. Religion does not give anyone power to change his or her circumstances. John the Baptist, the forerunner of Jesus, pronounced that all should repent, for the *Kingdom* of heaven was at hand. Jesus followed with the identical message of the Kingdom of heaven. Jesus was not a politician. He was not a prime minister or president, and He surely was not a religious leader. These titles do not exist in the Kingdom of God. Jesus Christ is King of kings, the Lord of lords, and High Priest to His people.

When He walked the earth, He spoke only *truth*, and the religious leaders couldn't handle it. He didn't preach about healing or deliverance; there was no need to preach or teach about it. In the *Kingdom*, healing is His children's bread; they just receive it by faith. Today, the message of the *Kingdom* has been shifted to many things: to the ministry of healing, prosperity, deliverance, pleasing people, and sowing a seed. That is why, when *truth* comes, very few want to hear it; they have already been grounded in different belief systems.

John 8:31–32 (NKJV) says, "Then Jesus said to those Jews who believed Him, 'If you abide in My word, you are My disciples indeed. And you shall know the truth, and the truth shall make you free.'" Our answers to many questions must bear the hallmark of honesty. We must take responsibility for what we have become and the things we have tolerated that have changed our community and nation. Moreover, we must be committed to integrity and character in every aspect of our lives; our lives in public and behind closed doors must be the same. Let us be a people confident that what we have done in the dark could be defended in the light. The world has change drastically from the time it was created, but the *Word of God* has not changed and will not change for anyone's conveniences.

God is not a human that He will lie. His values and principles remain the same in whatever country or continent you are living in.

Today in this crucial time and age, we do not need another politician who continues to lie to the people of the nation and gives false promises and hope, and is elected because of his or her covetousness behavior and filthy greed for money and power. We need *true leaders* who are willing to bring about the necessary *transformation* in the land for the betterment of the people and the nation. Consider the late Mr. Nelson Mandela who spent twenty-seven years in prison for human values. He was a man of *principles* and was not afraid to go to prison to bring liberation to his people and country. After being released from prison, Mr. Mandela became president of his nation. After serving one term, he walked away from politics with his principles and values intact. He became an example for many to follow, especially politicians.

Mr. Mandela didn't lay down his principles or the things that he believes in on the altar of compromise, as many politicians and so-called ministers of the gospel are doing today. He didn't pursue power but service to his people. He didn't look at power as a great privilege to better himself, his family, and his friends. He saw it as an opportunity to bring about *changes* and to leave a *legacy*. Then, people who took his place would be able to have principles and values as guidelines for continuing to do what was right for the betterment of the people and the nation.

That's why after his death and on the day of his burial, many *dignitaries* from all over the world could have taken the time to travel to South Africa and pay their final respects to a great man of the soil. Mr. Mandela will be remembered for his sacrifices, his determination to bring change and freedom for his people, his contribution to humanity, the life he lived, and the legacy he left behind for others to build upon.

You, too, can become a great man or woman of *God* and serve a greater purpose spiritually. Imagine God using you in your country to bring about an awakening for a day of repentance for *national transformation* and *revival*. Because of your submission in obedience to God, this change took place. Then, suddenly, a domino effect occurred, and the surrounding nations were also impacted. Revivals and deliverance occurred all over the world and millions came to know *Jesus Christ as Lord and Savior.* It is possible! Are you willing to pay the price and subject yourself to all that's necessary to bring about changes for the betterment of humanity? Your answer should be, "Yes, I am!" It is possible.

You might be considered or looked upon as insignificant in the eyes of people. What people think about you is not important; what God thinks about you is the most important. When we hide ourselves in God, He causes us to discover ourselves and the hidden treasures laid up inside of us. Only God that can carry us in places that we ourselves cannot. That's why it's important for us to be sold out to God to accomplish His will, purpose, and plans for our lives, and to be *true leaders* and exemplars to our family, our friends, and the communities where we live and minister.

When you seem insignificant in the eyes of people, they don't want to be close to you. Suddenly, God steps into your circumstances, changes them for your good, and brings a smile to your face. Then, everybody wants to get to know you. For God is about not only to promote but to *embarrass you with His blessings.* In your wildest moments, you may wonder what you have done to deserve all of this. Trust and obey God at His word. Declare over your life that you are an *agent* of change, and then do what God has called you to do. Step out in faith and trust God. When you can't trace His hands, trust His heart.

When a *true leader* walks and lives his or her life in integrity and character, he or she does not hurt other people. The person's character will be the defining mechanism in how he or she treats and respects the people who surround that person and who that person loves. The *character* of the individual will protect his or her entire future and allow him or her to enter the Kingdom of God.

Information doesn't bring transformation; conversion does.

Conversion is the initial change of attitude that brings a person into a right relationship with God. Therefore, conversion is more than the exchange of one set of beliefs for another; it is a *wholehearted turning to God*. That is why you must make the *Word of God* your standard of living. You must conform to it, take advice from it, and in everything be overruled and determined by it. Those who choose not to live according to the *Word of God* say there is no light, and they have no right sense of thinking. They also do not understand themselves or the difference between good and evil, truth and falsehood.

Those who reject divine revelation do not have much human understanding. They will be driven into darkness and despair where the worm dies not, and the fire is not quenched. Eternity is a long time to spend in the wrong place.

John said in Revelation 21:5–8 (NKJV),

> Then He who sat on the throne said, "Behold, I make all things new." And He said to me, "Write, for these words are true and faithful." And He said to me, "It is done! I am the Alpha and the Omega, the Beginning, and the End. I will give of the fountain of the water of life freely to him who thirsts. He who overcomes shall inherit all things, and I will be his God and he shall be My son. But the cowardly, unbelieving, abominable, murderers, sexually immoral, sorcerers, idolaters, and all liars shall have their part in the lake which burns with fire and brimstone, which is the second death.

Will you be restored to your maker before it's too late?

RELIGION IN THE PULPITS AND IN THE PEWS

(OPERATING IN GIFTS BUT ILLEGAL)

As we investigate the issues plaguing our heavenly Father's business, which have crept into it beginning hundreds of years ago and lasting even to this very day, we discover the main culprit is our enemy, the devil. Jesus said in Matthew 13:24–30 and 37–42, in relation to the tares and the wheat, that they must grow together; they are like identical twins. To know the difference, you must be a fruit inspector, for not everyone in the church belongs to the Lord Jesus Christ. That's why it's important as a true believer in Jesus to become a student of the Word of God, to pray and fast, and to be a true worshipper of Jehovah. This is the correct order. You need to set aside time to study scriptures for yourself. Ask the Holy Spirit to teach you, to bridge the gap from the natural to the supernatural, and to bring clarity and revelation as you avail yourself of the Word. When you go to church and when your pastor or a visiting pastor opens his or her mouth to preach, you will know if the pastor is preaching truth or lies.

In Matthew 7:24–27, Jesus describes two people with different foundations: the one who hears, understands, does His Word, and builds his or her house on the rock, and the other who hears and understands but fails to apply it and builds on sand. That's why He encourages you to lay a foundation in your life with the Word of God; it is the rock. Your soul and destiny are too important to entrust to the hands of your pastor (or whatever title he or she might be holding).

Another issue in the church is wrong interpretations of scriptures. This plays a major role in the downfall of the church today. Men and women say that they are called and anointed by God, but they still purpose in their hearts to manipulate and bewitch the very souls of the men and women with whom they have been entrusted. They bring about wrong interpretation of scriptures for their own selfish gain. They read into the Word that which is not theirs. Many times, they approach a passage of scripture thinking they already understand it and, in the process, they read their own meaning into the passage. This is called *eisegesis* (*eis* is a Greek preposition meaning "into").

Interpreting the Bible correctly demands that we listen to what the text itself is saying; then we can draw the meaning out of the passage. This is called *exegesis* (*ex* is a Greek preposition meaning "out of"). If we let a passage be defined by what it and the surrounding verses say, then we have taken a large step toward interpreting the Bible correctly. Only by watching the context carefully and by letting the passage speak for itself do we give scripture the respect it deserves. You might tell yourself it's impossible to interpret the Bible accurately. No, it's not impossible.

Acts 18:24–26 speaks of a certain Jew named Apollo, an eloquent man and mighty in scriptures. He was fervent in spirit, and spoke and taught accurately the things of the Lord, though he knew only the baptism of John. It is essential to recognize that the purpose and goal of study of scriptures is a godly life. Study is not complete until you put into practice what you have learned. The question to ask at this stage of interpretation is how you can apply what you have learned to how you live your life.

Tares and wheat growing together, wrong interpretation of scriptures over hundreds of years, and religion have become cancers in the church, and many are afraid to speak of them today. Has the Word of God changed from then to now? No. What's the problem?

Today, the spirit of religion has taken over many pulpits and pews, all because of the love of money. This book will be a reminder to you so you, too, can speak of it. It's our Father's business, and His business is about souls, not making money.

Being a true son of my Father, I am concerned. Imposters are standing behind the pulpits, wolves in sheep's clothing, and someone must speak. I choose to speak instead of remaining quiet. If I don't speak, then I accept everything that's happening in the church; I refuse to accept anything that is not of God.

Religion in the church did not start yesterday; it started in the Old Testament era. As we investigate the best information available for us today, for it is foolproof, let us therefore unfold the Word of God. In Numbers 21:4–9, the Jews became weary and discouraged after their journey. They spoke against God and his servant Moses, saying, "Have you brought us here to die in this place? There's no food and water for our children and us. Why didn't you just leave us in Egypt?" They were a bunch of ungrateful covenant individuals. Their attitude caused the Jews to sin, and the Lord sent a fiery serpent to chastise the people for their disobedience. Whomever the serpent bit eventually died.

After a while, the people approached Moses and cried out, "For we have sinned." They repented, begged for deliverance, and said, "Pray to the Lord for us that He will remove the serpents from among us." Moses prayed, and the Lord heard him. The Lord commanded him to make a fiery serpent out of bronze material. Moses did as the Lord instructed him; he made the fiery serpent and set it on a pole. Whenever someone who was bitten looked at the bronze fiery serpent, that person lived and did not die.

It didn't stop there. When the Israelites entered the land of Canaan, they carried the bronze serpent with them and preserved it for many years until the reign of Hezekiah, king of Judah. Second Kings 18:1–6 tells us that during his reformation throughout the nation, Hezekiah destroyed the bronze serpent image that Moses, the Lord's servant, made because it had been turned into an instrument for idol worship. The people took a righteous instrument used to bring deliverance from death and turned it into an idol. This caused their hearts to shift from serving the true, living God to existing in a state of idolatry, which became spiritual adultery.

Hezekiah trusted in the Lord, and there was none like him among all the kings of Judah who were before or after him. He held fast to the Lord, did not depart from following Him, and kept His commandments, which the Lord had given to Moses. Hezekiah lived a blameless life to the very end. What about you? Are you willing to serve God faithfully to the end despite what befalls you?

John 3:14 (NKJV) says, "And as Moses lifted the serpent in the wilderness, even so must the Son of Man be lifted." Just as the bronze serpent brought deliverance from death from the poisonous snakes, so the Son of Man must be lifted to deliver humanity from sin. As the Israelites had to look in faith at the bronze fiery serpent to be saved from death, so must we look in faith to Jesus Christ only, not humankind, to have eternal life.

Today in the church, it's no different. Men and women are being used by God as instruments of righteousness to bring about healing and deliverance in the lives of humanity. However, most of them eventually lose focus because they have allowed the people to place and keep them on pedestals. These are the same people who have received healing or deliverance and are sitting right in the pews in the church. That feeling of great importance and glory is a dangerous thing; the devil tried it with Jesus in Luke 4:5–7, and he didn't succeed. Romans 15:4 and 1 Corinthians 10:1 were written for our learning and admonition. Why do men and women continue to fall prey to these very things we were warned of? The answer to this question is in Hosea 4:6; most church folks are too lazy to search the scriptures for themselves. There's no spiritual growth in their lives for they love to depend on their pastor to teach them.

While tares and wheat will grow together until the time of harvest, it's important for you to be very careful in these evil days we are living in. Jesus said in Matthew 7:21–23 (NKJV),

> Not everyone who says to Me, Lord, Lord, shall enter the kingdom of heaven, but he who does the will of My Father in heaven. Many will say to Me on that day, Lord, have we not prophesied in Your name, cast out demons in Your name, and done many wonders in Your name? And then I will declare to them, I never knew you; depart from Me, you who practice lawlessness.

You might not know because in some ministries, gifts are the assurance that the Holy Spirit is there. No! Gifts are no assurance. When God gives you a gift, He doesn't take it back. Job said, "The Lord gave and the Lord hath taken away; blessed be the Lord" (Job 1:21). Job only had a mere knowledge of Jehovah but needed an encounter with God to understand who God really is. Jesus said, "You will know them by their fruits, not their gifts" (Matthew 7:16). He also said, "Many will come to me on that day and say, 'Have we not prophesied, cast out devils, and done many wonders in Your name?'" Then Jesus will say, "I never knew you" (Matthew 7:22–23). Let me assure you that the Holy Spirit will leave you when you are not abiding in the Father's will. He leaves you with the gifts because the Lord doesn't take back what He gives to you, because the Holy Spirit is a person.

These said people have tolerated religion and manipulation. They have bewitched the people and allowed underhanded involvement to take place in the church because of their selfish greed. They will lose it all. Even their very souls will end up in hell if they don't repent and come back to the Lord Jesus Christ.

John said in Revelation 3:20 (NKJV), "Behold, I stand at the door and knock. If anyone hears My voice and opens the door, I will come into him and dine with him, and he with Me." I want you to understand this verse. The Lord was knocking at the heart of humankind in the Laodicean church; if He was in the church, would He have to knock at the heart of humankind? No! This means that the Holy Spirit wasn't there. That church was called to repent before it was too late.

Eli was a judge and high priest with whom the prophet Samuel lived with during his childhood. Samuel's mother, Hannah by name, was childless and poured out her heart to the Lord because of her unhappiness. Her prayers for a son were heard and answered. The Lord granted her heart's desire because she vowed to give her son back to the service of the Lord. The Lord wanted someone to represent Him to the people because the priesthood was corrupt. When Samuel was born, his mother was true to her word: she brought him to the tabernacle and dedicated him to the Lord. There the prophet of the Lord lived with the high priest Eli.

Eli was a pious man whose service to the Lord was unblemished; however, he was lax as a father toward his two sons and had no control over them. Hophni and Phinehas took meat from the sacrificial animals before they were dedicated to God. They also lay with the women who assembled at the door of the tabernacle in 1 Samuel 2:22 NKJV: "Now Eli was very old; and he heard everything his sons did to all Israel, and how they lay with the women who assembled at the door of the tabernacle of meeting." God pronounced judgment on Eli because of his failure to discipline his sons.

God's judgment was carried out through the Philistines. Eli's two sons Hophni and Phinehas carried the Ark of the Covenant into the tent of the Israelites to help with the battle. When the Ark came, the people shouted and the whole earth shook, but the Lord was not in their midst. Not all shouts prove that God is in the midst. Both brothers were killed, and the Ark was captured. Eli, ninety-eight years old and nearly blind, heard the news. The messenger told Eli that Israel had fled before the Philistines, and there had been a great slaughter among the people. He also told Eli his two sons were dead and the Ark of God had been captured. When the messenger mentioned the Ark of God, Eli fell off the seat backward by the side of the gate. His neck was broken and he died, for he was old and heavy. He had judged Israel for forty years.

Eli's sons proved unworthy of priestly duties; their behavior was characterized by greed, lust, and immorality. Eli made only a halfhearted attempt to control his son's scandalous behavior. Consequently, God's judgment was pronounced upon Eli and his entire lineage. When Phinehas's wife heard the news, she went into premature labor and died in childbirth. The child was named Ichabod, which means the glory has departed from Israel. Because of the evil actions of Phinehas and Hophni, the high priesthood later passed from Eli's family to another.

What happened to Eli, his sons, and their entire lineage to prevent them from continuing in the service of the priesthood? This is just an avenue God chose to stop the tolerance of wickedness in His business. God is good, but He's not clueless; the longest rope has an end.

Today in the church, the important thing is who has the bigger building, who has the better preacher, who could lead worship better, who has the bigger congregation, and so on. There is competition in the church. They behave just like the religious folks of the many religions in existence.

They forgot whose work it is, and who made them the overseers before they became corrupted. These people state they started this work, forgetting this work started nearly two thousand years ago. How old are you? Are you the founder of the ministry? Whose words are you using to teach and preach to the people? Do you have the Holy Spirit to give freely to the people? If your answer to these questions is no, why don't you repent and come back into alignment with God before you end up like Eli and his sons. The Lord's work and business are not your family business, so stop treating it so. You ought not to be in ministry for your selfish gain, but for the love of souls.

The church is far from being one and we are the ones who have the truth. For many in the church, both ministers and lay people, their characters and integrity are shallow. We are competing against ourselves and no one wins. We forget we are not in a religion but in the Kingdom of God. Are we living according to the truth? Do we have knowledge of who God is and ignorantly serve Him, believing we are in right standing with Him? On the other hand, do you like Job? Job only had knowledge of God until he had an *encounter with God*. Do you need an encounter also?

In religion, the people fight. In the church, people fighting because they are the tares which Jesus spoke about. Everyone wants to make an everlasting or famous name for himself or herself. It started at the Tower of Babel and continues today in politics, in acting, in religion, and even in the church—yes, the church; that shouldn't be a surprise. Men and women who called themselves servants of Jesus Christ have lost focus and are missing the mark of the higher calling.

Jesus never pursued fame or popularity, and neither did the apostles. John 6 tells us that one day after Jesus performed a miracle, the people had a wicked intention. Jesus perceived the wickedness in their hearts and ran away. They wanted to make Him king by force. What Jesus ran away from, many in the church are running toward.

The safest way to make a name without compromising your calling is to remain submitted to God. He who humbles himself shall be exalted, but he who exalts himself shall be abased. When you submit to authority, you don't have to promote yourself; ask Abraham. You don't have to pay a preacher to have a meeting because he is well known all over. Maybe the preacher is a well-known talk show host who can showcase you on radio or television. That is called seeking the wrong avenue to bring self-gratification through a bootleg promotion. Instead of being promoted, you will be demoted. In God's Kingdom, you don't promote yourself; the King promotes you. Amen.

What's going on around us today, not only in the church but in the world? In the church, there are religious folks who profess to know Jesus. Religion has a great hold on humanity for it has been in existence nearly 4000 years. That's why people say they were born Hindu, or Muslim, or Catholic, or Christian because their parents were of certain religions. Every one of them who made such a statement and continues to make such a statement needs Jesus. Everyone was born a sinner. Psalm 51:5 (NKJV) says, "Behold, I was brought forth in iniquity, and in sin my mother conceived me." Most of the people in the church came from different religious beliefs and backgrounds. Their previous religions and gods could not have helped them or given them the power to change their circumstances. They said, "Let us try another God whose name is Jesus, for nothing is wrong in trying him. He's just another God." Jesus changed their circumstances and saved them, but they have not been delivered in their minds as yet. They are still holding on to religious beliefs, traditions, and teachings from their ancestors. There are strongholds in their lives that manipulate the way they think. It becomes easy for them to put their pastors on pinnacles because that is where their pundits were. They strongly need deliverance from that spirit of foolishness. Religion and tradition are very difficult to release.

Acts 6:5 speaks of the selection of seven deacons. The last one was Nicolas, a proselyte from Antioch. Nicolas introduced a doctrine in the early church that Jesus Himself hated. Revelations 2:6 (AMP) states, "Yet you have this to your credit], that you hate the works and corrupt teachings of the Nicolaitans [that mislead and delude the people, which I also hate." The doctrine of the Nicolaitans is that you can have one foot in church and the other in the world. It is a teaching of idolatry that always leads to spiritual adultery.

Jesus said He came not to destroy the law or the prophets but to fulfill it. The fulfillment of the law is that anyone or anything you put before Jehovah is idolatry. In the New Testament period, the term *idolatry* became more than bowing down before a statue; it came to mean replacing God in the mind and heart of the worshiper. Ephesians 5:5 and Colossians 3:5 point in this direction. The believer must put to death covetousness, which is idolatry. The believer must understand the vicious nature of idolatry.

While we may not make or bow down to a statue, we must be constantly on guard that we let nothing and no one come between God and us. As soon as anything does, it becomes an idol.

When speaking of Himself as the Good Shepherd in John 10:11–15, Jesus indicates that He has a personal interest in His sheep (his followers), unlike a hireling, who watches over the sheep for a salary. Many go into ministry for a salary and not because they are called. They see an opportunity and an easy way to make money. Jesus says He is the Good Shepherd and He gives His life for the sheep. He does not merely speak about love but expresses His love to and for people. Imposters who call themselves anointed by the Lord are really imposters of the faith. They continue to use sheep as walls to protect themselves. Isn't the responsibility of a good shepherd to tend, to feed the truth of the *Word of God*, and to protect, strengthen, and discipline the sheep?

These ministers who are using sheep as bodyguards are afraid to die because they don't know how to trust in God for their protection. They trust in their own security, for they don't belong to Him. They have become like religious Peter in the garden of Gethsemane when he drew his sword to protect Jesus. Jesus didn't need his protection. Religion deals with violence and insecurity. The only way these hireling and false ministers can keep their big followings is through manipulation and bewitching of the people. They refuse to turn to God for mercy and to give up that kind of living. They are not ready to leave behind their wealth. It's not a problem for them to use sheep as shields to protect themselves. There's no love for the souls of people but there is love for mammon.

Their message of the kingdom of heaven has changed to miracle and money services. Thousands attend these services. After the healing and deliverance have come to an end, the minister will use one of his or her favorite portions of scripture, taken from 2 Chronicles

20:20: "Believe in the Lord your God, so shall you be established; believe his prophets, so shall ye prosper." That means it's time for people to sow seeds and to continue finding favor with God and to keep their healing. That's spiritual manipulation. The devil is a liar. Did Jesus ever imply after He healed, delivered, or set anyone free that he or she should sow a seed? No, He didn't. Instead, He told them to go and sin no more. They did not need to sow any seed to keep their healing. That's why the Lord said in Hosea 4:6, "My people are destroyed for a lack of knowledge." Ignorance is the enemy of the kingdom of God. May God have mercy on His people, for it's better to be a servant in heaven, than a king in hell.

The time has come to unmask the deception of false ministers who call themselves the Lord's anointed but are enemies of the cross. They are leading millions away from the presence and purposes of God. God is looking for a John the Baptist who is not afraid to speak out against unrighteousness in the church. Will you answer the call?

It truly amazes me that, when corruption in politics is discovered, the authorities step in and take proper measures to bring the culprit or culprits to justice. In the church, the people remain silent, forgetting that silence is a voice for approval of what's happening in that place of worship. May the Father of Spirits continue to have mercy upon His people. As Paul said in 2 Timothy 3:13 (AMP), "But wicked men and imposters will go on from bad to worse, deceiving and leading astray others and being deceived and led astray themselves."

As someone once said,

> The church began as a movement in Jerusalem. It became a philosophy in Greece, an institution in Rome, and a culture in Europe. When it came to the United States of America, it became a moneymaking business. It is a highly profitable business, but God is coming back for a movement.

Scriptures for Reading and Admonition

Therefore, you shepherds, hear the word of the
LORD: As surely as I live, says the Sovereign LORD,
you abandoned my flock and left them to be attacked
by every wild animal. And though you were my
shepherds, you didn't search for my sheep when they
were lost. You took care of yourselves and left the
sheep to starve. Therefore, you shepherds, hear the
word of the LORD. This is what the Sovereign LORD
says: I now consider these shepherds my enemies, and
I will hold them responsible for what has happened
to my flock. I will take away their right to feed the
flock, and I will stop them from feeding themselves.
I will rescue my flock from their mouths; the sheep
will no longer be their prey. (Ezekiel 34:7–10 NLT)

All you beasts of the field, come to devour, All you
beasts in the forest. His watchmen are blind, they
are all ignorant; They are all dumb dogs, they cannot
bark; Sleeping, lying down, loving to slumber. Yes,
they are greedy dogs Which never have enough.
And they are shepherds Who cannot understand;
They all look to their own way, Everyone for his
own gain, From his own territory. "Come," one says,
"I will bring wine, and we will fill ourselves with
intoxicating drink; Tomorrow will be as today, And
much more abundant." (Isaiah 56:9–12 NKJV)

And indeed, now I know that you all, among whom
I have gone preaching the kingdom of God, will see
my face no more. Therefore I testify to you this day
that I am innocent of the blood of all men. For I have
not shunned to declare to you the whole counsel of

God. Therefore take heed to yourselves and to all the flock, among which the Holy Spirit has made you overseers, to shepherd the church of God which He purchased with His own blood. For I know this, that after my departure savage wolves will come in among you, not sparing the flock. Also from among yourselves men will rise up, speaking perverse things, to draw away the disciples after themselves. Therefore watch and remember that for three years I did not cease to warn everyone night and day with tears. (Acts 20:25–31 NKJV)

Now the Spirit expressly says that in latter times some will depart from the faith, giving heed to deceiving spirits and doctrines of demons, Speaking lies in hypocrisy, having their own conscience seared with a hot iron. (1 Timothy 4:1–2 NKJV)

If the Lord Jesus is willing, I hope to send Timothy to you soon for a visit. Then he can cheer me up by telling me how you are getting along. I have no one else like Timothy, who genuinely cares about your welfare. All the others care only for themselves and not for what matters to Jesus Christ. (Philippians 2:19–21 NLT)

Look to God's instructions and teachings! People who contradict his word are completely in the dark. (Isaiah 8:20 NLT)

But why do you call Me Lord, Lord, and not do the things which I say? (Luke 6:46 NKJV)

Then Jesus said to His disciples, "If anyone wishes to follow Me [as My disciple], he must deny himself [set aside selfish interests] and take up his cross [expressing a willingness to endure whatever may come] and follow Me [believing in Me, conforming to My example in living and, if need be, suffering or perhaps dying because of faith in Me]. For whoever wishes to save his life [in this world] will [eventually] lose it [through death], but whoever loses his life [in this world] for My sake will find it [that is, life with Me for all eternity]. For what will it profit a man if he gains the whole world [wealth, fame, success], but forfeits his soul? Or what will a man give in exchange for his soul? (Matthew 16:24–26 AMP)

Then the seventy returned with joy, saying, "Lord, even the demons are subject to us in Your name." And He said to them, "I saw Satan fall like lightning from heaven. Behold, I give you the authority to trample on serpents and scorpions, and over all the power of the enemy, and nothing shall by any means hurt you. Nevertheless do not rejoice in this, that the spirits are subject to you, but rather rejoice because your names are written in heaven. (Luke 10:17–20 NKJV)

Whoever says he lives in Christ [that is, whoever says he has accepted Him as God and Savior] ought [as a moral obligation] to walk and conduct himself just as He walked and conducted Himself. (1 John 2:6 AMP)

And you shall be holy to Me, for I the Lord am holy, and have separated you from the peoples, that you should be Mine. (Leviticus 20:26 NKJV)

Pursue peace with all people, and holiness, without which no one will see the Lord. (Hebrews 12:14 NKJV)

This Book of the Law shall not depart from your mouth, but you shall meditate in it day and night, that you may observe to do according to all that is written in it. For then you will make your way prosperous, and then you will have good success. (Joshua 1:8 NKJV)

I am astonished and extremely irritated that you are so quickly shifting your allegiance and deserting Him who called you by the grace of Christ, for a different [even contrary] gospel; Which is really not another [gospel]; but there are [obviously] some [people masquerading as teachers] who are disturbing and confusing you [with a misleading, counterfeit teaching] and want to distort the gospel of Christ [twisting it into something which it absolutely is not]. But even if we, or an angel from heaven, should preach to you a gospel contrary to that which we [originally] preached to you, let him be condemned to destruction! As we have said before, so I now say again, if anyone is preaching to you a gospel different from that which you received [from us], let him be condemned to destruction! Am I now trying to win the favor and approval of men, or of God? Or am I seeking to please someone? If I were still trying to be popular with men, I would not be a bondservant of Christ. (Galatians 1:6–10 AMP)

For I testify to everyone who hears the words of the prophecy of this book: If anyone adds to these things, God will add to him the plagues that are written in this book; And if anyone takes away from the words of the book of this prophecy, God shall take away his part from the Book of Life, from the holy city, and from the things which are written in this book. (Revelation 22:18–19 NKJV)

For whoever wishes to save his life [in this world] will [eventually] lose it [through death], but whoever loses his life [in this world] for My sake, he is the one who will save it [from the consequences of sin and separation from God]. (Luke 9:24 AMP)

THE DIFFERENCE BETWEEN RELIGION AND THE KINGDOM OF GOD

Today, we are going to take a little journey back into history a few thousand years so we will understand the difference between religion and the Kingdom of God. This journey will enable you, the reader, to make the best decision you will ever make in your life if you don't know Jesus as Lord. The road you are on is not about a religion but the Kingdom of God.

The scriptures say in Romans 15:4 (NKJV), "For whatever things were written before were written for our learning, that we through the patience and comfort of the Scriptures might have hope."

We did not exist when it all happened, but there's information set aside for us to understand what took place in that era when religion and the thousands of different languages came into existence because of disobedience. We must understand that religion did not exist before the great flood of Noah. Before the flood, there was a form of godliness and truth but also denial of their power. The Bible mentions Noah in Genesis chapters 5 and 6. Noah found grace in the eyes of the Lord.

God purposed that He would destroy humanity because of its wickedness and callous behavior upon the earth. The same God who created you and me purposed in His heart that He would destroy our ancestors. When God created humans in the garden, they were created with purpose. Because of sin and disobedience, the hearts of humans have turned away from their God and Maker, Jehovah by name. After time had elapsed and humankind had increased upon the earth, wickedness and immoral behavior increased also. However, Noah found *grace* in the eyes of his Maker. Because of him, his entire house was saved and spared from the dreadful death that was coming upon the earth. His family built the ark and entered it for the preservation of life, and for God's will and purpose to become a reality, which God has promised. Genesis 3:15 (NKJV) says, "And I will put enmity between you and the woman, and between your seed and her Seed; he shall bruise your head, and you shall bruise his heel."

After the flood, the Lord gave Noah the same commands recorded in Genesis 9:1 (NKJV): "So, God blessed Noah and his sons, and said to them: 'Be fruitful and multiply and fill the earth.'"

In relation to our first parents, "God blessed them, and God said to them, 'Be fruitful and multiply; fill the earth and subdue it; have dominion over the fish of the sea, over the birds of the air, and over every living thing that moves on the earth'" (Genesis 1:28 NKJV).

After the flood, the family of Noah increased in an unnumbered multitude over a period of time. Genesis 11:1–9 (AMP) records when religion began. The tower of Babel symbolizes human pride and rebellion against Jehovah God.

> Now the whole earth spoke one language and used the same words (vocabulary). And as people journeyed eastward, they found a plain in the land of Shinar and they settled there. They said one to another, "Come, let us make bricks and fire them thoroughly [in a kiln, to harden and strengthen them]." So, they used brick for stone [as building material], and they used tar (bitumen, asphalt) for mortar. They said, "Come, let us build a city for ourselves, and a tower whose top will reach into

the heavens, and let us make a [famous] name for ourselves, so that we will not be scattered [into separate groups] and be dispersed over the surface of the entire earth [as the LORD instructed]. Now the LORD came down to see the city and the tower which the sons of men had built. And the LORD said, "Behold, they are one [unified] people, and they all have the same language. This is only the beginning of what they will do [in rebellion against Me], and now no evil thing they imagine they can do will be impossible for them. Come, let Us (Father, Son, Holy Spirit) go down and there confuse and mix up their language, so that they will not understand one another's speech. So the LORD scattered them abroad from there over the surface of the entire earth; and they stopped building the city. Therefore the name of the city was Babel—because there the LORD confused the language of the entire earth; and from that place the LORD scattered and dispersed them over the surface of all the earth.

First, the descendants of Noah were united by the strong bond of a common language and were unwilling to separate because they were one. They came upon a plain in the land of Shinar and dwelt there. They built themselves a city and a tower because they wanted to reach the heavens and make great and everlasting names for themselves. Many do this today in politics, in acting, in religion, and even in the church. Yes, the church shouldn't be a surprise. Future generations would know that there had been such people in the world. They did not want to die and leave no memorials behind them. However, to do this would have defeated the command of God to be fruitful, multiply, and fill the earth. Attempting to prevent emigration was foolish, and wicked.

To the inferiority of human pride, the tower was a skyscraper.

To the Father of spirits, it was so small that He had to come down from heaven to catch a glimpse of this tiny, meaningless effort of His creation. The construction of the tower and city is described as evil and an act of self-glorification by the builders. God said that whatever they purposed to do they could accomplish because they were one and wanted to make a name for themselves. They sought their own security in community life independent of Him.

It is just for God to bury those names in the dust that are raised by sin. These Babel-builders put themselves to a great deal of foolish expense to make names for themselves. They could not gain even this point, for we do not find in any history books the name of so much as one of these builders. Jehovah allowed them to proceed in a good way in their construction before he put a stop to it. Then they could have space to repent. If not, their disappointment might be the more shameful.

It is only from scriptures we learn the true origin of the birthing of the different nations and languages of the world. Traditions, religions, cultures, and customs were birthed at the tower of Babel. Gods and different beliefs were formed there. The reason for this drastic move by God is found in verse 6. God had to do what He had to do because He said whatever evil they purposed or imagined in their hearts would not be impossible for them because they were one. Imagine all these people trying to fit within one community. There was space throughout the earth to form 196 countries and roughly 4500 different languages.

Their communication with each other to advance their efforts was frustrating because they began to speak different languages. Finally, they abandoned the building project of the tower and city and departed on their own ways. The language barrier God caused for them scattered them and fulfilled His commands. The children of humankind were now finally scattered abroad upon the face of the whole earth. They departed in companies after their families and after their tongues. They never did, nor ever will, all come together again until that great day. Matthew 25:31–33 (NKJV) states,

When the Son of Man comes in His glory, and all
the holy angels with Him, then He will sit on the
throne of His glory. All the nations will be gathered
before Him, and He will separate them one from
another, as a shepherd divides his sheep from the
goats. And He will set the sheep on His right hand,
but the goats on the left.

By one miracle of tongues, people were dispersed throughout the
earth and gradually fell away from relationship with their Maker.
By another miracle, national barriers from tongues were broken
down that all people might be brought back to the family of God.
Humankind does not need another religion but needs to come back to
its Maker and God. Over the thousands of years of human existence,
humans have not changed much. The human heart is still wicked and
deceitful. Only the working power of the Holy Spirit and submission
to God can change it.

The people purposely rebelled against God, knowing what they
were doing was against God's commands. Their ancestor Noah
passed on the commands he received from the Lord. When we look
back thousands of years ago to what happened and at what's going on
around us today, not only in the church but in the world, we see the
situation is worse now.

Religion has a great hold on humanity because it has been in
existence nearly 4000 years now. What will you do about it? Religion
does not give you hope of a better tomorrow. Religion causes you to
spend all your hard-earned money seeking answers where answers
are not found. Religion is a deception of the devil himself; we must
understand that we are more spiritual than physical beings. The spirit
could exist without your body, but your body cannot exist without the
spirit. The body is insignificant without the spirit. The Bible tells us
in Genesis 2:7 (NKJV), "And the Lord God formed man of the dust
of the ground and breathed into his nostrils the breath of life; and
man became a living being."

That's why as true believers in Christ Jesus, we ought not to hoard. When we die, we carry nothing with us. In some religions, they bury the dead with money, whether to sustain themselves in Purgatory or somewhere else I can't say. Purgatory is a religious word, and it plays a deceptive role for millions of people in that belief group. It is said to be a place where souls go after death. They wait for their loved ones to pay a lot of money for a mass so the priest can pray their souls into heaven. Now if that is true, and we know it's not, then what they are saying is that Jesus Christ died in vain. The devil is a liar, and their beliefs are lies.

The Bible tells me in Hebrews 9:27 (NKJV), "And as it is appointed for men to die once, but after this the judgment." There's no middle ground after death. Either you enter the presence of the Lord Jesus Christ or you go to hell. Which one depends on how you live your life and the choices you make on a daily basis. You choose either Jesus or Satan, holy or unholy living, or speaking truth or speaking lies. This life is not a game. Do not play with your destiny.

God's rejection of the nations symbolized by the tower of Babel is reversed in Genesis 12:1–3 by the call of Abram, through whom all nations would be blessed. The diversity of human language, as described in this account, had Pentecost as its answer. On that day, the Holy Spirit was poured out on the people in the upper room. They started speaking in unknown tongues. They understood one another although they spoke different languages. Acts 2:1–12 says the barriers that divided people and nations were thus removed. Amen.

Genesis 9:20–27 (NKJV) informs us why Jehovah chose and called Abram out of one nation and tongue: so that His purpose, will, and promise would continue to become a reality.

> And Noah began to be a farmer, and he planted a vineyard. Then he drank of the wine and was drunk and became uncovered in his tent. And

Ham, the father of Canaan, saw the nakedness of his father, and told his two brothers outside. But Shem and Japheth took a garment, laid it on both their shoulders, and went backward and covered the nakedness of their father. Their faces were turned away, and they did not see their father's nakedness. So Noah awoke from his wine and knew what his younger son had done to him. Then he said: "Cursed be Canaan; A servant of servants He shall be to his brethren." And he said: "Blessed be the Lord, The God of Shem, and may Canaan be his servant. May God enlarge Japheth, and may he dwell in the tents of Shem; And may Canaan be his servant.

Noah became a farmer after the flood. He planted a vineyard, made wine, and got so drunk that he removed his clothing and became naked. Alcohol disturbs the way you think and brings you into a place of unawareness to do whatever is displeasing to your own self. The vineyard became a stumbling block in Noah's life. This is the first time the scriptures mention Noah drinking alcohol. One of Noah son's saw him naked and, instead of covering his nakedness, he told his siblings about it. In reality, Ham looked upon the nakedness of his mother also when he refused to cover his father. When Noah became sober and awoke from his drunkenness, he understood what Ham had done. He pronounced a curse upon Ham's lineage because Ham looked upon the nakedness of his parents. (Read Leviticus chapters 18 through 20.)

After Noah cursed the lineage of Ham, he pronounced a blessing upon the two other sons. Shem received the greatest blessing (verse 26). I pronounced the very blessing Shem received over your life and your household because you have purchased this book and have encouraged others to buy a copy also. I bless you in Jesus's name. Receive it by faith. Amen.

Genesis 11:10–26 teaches us that from Shem to Abram is ten generations. That's why Abram was called by Jehovah God in Genesis 12:1–3 (NKJV).

> Now the Lord had said to Abram: "Get out of your country, from your family and from your father's house to a land that I will show you. I will make you a great nation; I will bless you and make your name great; and you shall be a blessing. I will bless those who bless you, and I will curse him who curses you; and in you all the families of the earth shall be blessed.

Abram was a descendent of Shem. When Shem was blessed by Noah, Abram was in his loins. That's why God only operated according to the blessing pronounced on Shem. God's plan to redeem humankind can continue in accordance with the promise He made in Genesis 3:15.

God promised Abram many good things only if he would obey Him. What stands out of all the promises is the very thing humans yearn for, both then and now. God said, "I will make your name great." Abram obeyed God and all the promises became his. He became a friend of God because of his love for and obedience to his Maker.

■ ■ ■

In 1 Kings 18:15–40, a public trial was about to take place on Mount Carmel between the servant of Jehovah and the servants of Baal. Each had to present evidence, and whoever could not would be put to death.

When Ahab the king saw Elijah, he accused him of causing trouble for Israel. However, Elijah said Ahab and his father's house had troubled Israel because they had forsaken the commandments of the Lord. Israel would no longer be troubled by them. Elijah summoned all of Israel and the prophets off Baal to Mount Carmel for a showdown. The God who answered by fire would be declared Lord over Israel. Elijah asked the people how long they would falter between two opinions. He charged the people for mixing the worship of God and the worship of Baal together, for they were unstable in their minds.

They worshipped God to please the prophets, but worshipped Baal to please Jezebel in order to be favored.

Elijah gave them an option. If Baal was God, they ought to renounce Jehovah and cleave to Baal only. If Jehovah was God, they must renounce Baal and serve Jehovah only. The people's hearts were divided, whereas Jehovah would have all or none. This was a fair proposal, but the people did not know what to say and answered him not a word. They could say nothing to justify or condemn themselves.

Elijah stood alone in the cause of God and said the God that answered by fire would be God. They readied their sacrifices. We may well imagine what a noise it was when 450 men began to cry out as one man with all their might, "O Baal! Hear us, O Baal! Answer us." This went on for some hours. Like fools, they leaped upon the altar as if they would also offer themselves as sacrifices. Because Baal was not answering them, they leaped up and down and danced about for some time hoping for a miracle. Like madmen, they cut themselves with knives and lancets, for it was their religious custom. They hoped the extra blood would appease Baal and he would hear their cry.

Elijah stood by them, mocking and telling them all sorts of things. He patiently waited for many hours. He heard them praying and doing all kinds of foolish things so their idol would hear them and bring down fire. Idols are meaningless and can neither save nor deliver anyone. Even though Satan is the prince and power of the air, the Lord did not permit him to bring down fire at that time. Revelation 13:13–14 (NKJV) says,

> He performs great signs, so that he even makes fire come down from heaven on the earth in the sight of men. And he deceives those who dwell on the

earth—by those signs which he was granted to do in the sight of the beast, telling those who dwell on the earth to make an image to the beast who was wounded by the sword and lived.

God would not suffer the devil to do it then because the trial of His title was put on that issue by the consent of the parties. The God who answers by *fire* is the true God. Satan cannot display great power unless Jehovah allows it; the devil must seek permission. An example is in the book of Job, chapters 1 and 2.

After the prophets of Baal had done all they could do, there was still no fire. Elijah found the ruins of a broken-down altar and repaired it with twelve stones according to the number of the twelve tribes of Israel. He brought the bullock and the wood for the sacrifice, but the Lord would provide the fire. If we sincerely offer our hearts to God, He will by His grace kindle a holy fire in them. Elijah was no priest and was not qualified to make an offering to the Lord according to the *laws of God*. Elijah had the power and the Lord gave him the authority to operate as a priest at the time. Elijah had to produce evidence because he was on trial because the God who answered by fire was the true God.

Elijah addressed himself to God by prayer before the altar. He humbly asked Him to accept the offering and to testify His acceptance of it by fire. His prayer was not long but precise. He used no vain repetitions. Though he expected an answer by fire, he came near to the altar with boldness and feared not. He addressed himself to God as the God of Abraham, Isaac, and Israel, exercising faith in the God of his ancestors. Elijah pleaded with the Lord to hear him and answer him so it would be known that He was God in Israel. Elijah said he was God's servant. He hoped that by this miracle, the hearts of the people would turn back to God. God answered him by fire while he was speaking, but this was not all. To complete the miracle, the fire consumed the stones of the altar and the very dust, demonstrating that it was no ordinary fire.

Elijah had by the most convincing and undeniable evidence proved his claims on behalf of the God of Israel. The people as the jury gave their verdict upon the trial. They agreed that the trial was fair, Baal was found guilty of being an imposter, and his servants were sentenced to death. The case was so plain that they did not need not to go from the bar to consider their verdict or consult about it. They fell on their faces and all as one said the Lord was God, not Baal. They saw the evidence and were convinced and satisfied. They declared that day and for all eternity that Jehovah alone was God in Israel and worthy of being praised. The 450 false prophets of Baal were seized and executed according to the law in Deuteronomy 13:1–5. The people needed no proof because all Israel witnessed what had happened. Therefore, Elijah ordered the prophets to be slain immediately as the troublers of the land.

■ ■ ■

The finality of it is that religion and Satan have no power over the King and His Kingdom.

Religion is the downfall of humanity. It has been used and continues to be used by Satan to bring destruction to humanity. However, it's not too late to change the road on which you are travelling.

The Bible says in Matthew 7:13–14 (NKJV), "Enter by the narrow gate; for wide is the gate and broad is the way that leads to destruction, and there are many who go in by it. Because narrow is the gate and difficult is the way which leads to life, and there are few who find it."

Before Jesus mentioned the descriptions and sizes of both destinies, He told you which one to choose. He cares and knows what's best for you. He is most concerned about where you will spend eternity. He made the choice for you even knowing you have the free will to choose. This was all because of His love for you—yes, you—and because He does not want you to spend eternity in the wrong place. Broad is the way that leads to *religion*—yes, religion. It brings destruction and havoc to all of humanity. In religion, any and every form of immoral way of living is accepted: adultery, fornication, sorcery, telling lies, same sex marriage, idolatry, stealing, hatred, and many other things. Many will follow that path because it's easy to live that kind of life without conviction.

The narrow gateway that leads to Kingdom living requires holiness, speaking truth, abiding in the constitution that governs it (the *Word of God*) uprightness, purity in heart, walking in the fear of God, marriage between one man and one woman, living a life of love for your neighbors, and many other values and principles laid down in scriptures. It's the only way to live because it displays the nature and character of my *King Jesus*.

Acts 10:38 (NKJV) says, "How God anointed Jesus of Nazareth with the Holy Spirit and with power, who went about doing good and healing all who were oppressed by the devil, for God was with Him."

■ ■ ■

God's ideal for the family is that it be a harmonious unit, where love for God and neighbors is instilled into each member (Deuteronomy 6:6–9). If the couple is divided, especially over religious beliefs, they can never have the harmony and sense of common purpose that God desires. Therefore, Old Testament believers were instructed not to marry foreigners who would hinder their faith and bring strife to the marriage (Exodus 34:13–16; Deuteronomy 7:3–6). Likewise, the apostle Paul commanded the New Testament believers, "Do not be unequally yoked together with unbelievers" (2 Corinthians 6:14–18; 7:1).

Scriptures for Reading and Admonition

> And these words which I command you today shall be in your heart. You shall teach them diligently to your children and shall talk of them when you sit in your house, when you walk by the way, when you lie down, and when you rise up. You shall bind them as a sign on your hand, and they shall be as frontlets between your eyes. You shall write them on the doorposts of your house and on your gates. (Deuteronomy 6:6–9 NKJV)

> But you shall destroy their altars, break their sacred pillars, and cut down their wooden images (For you shall worship no other god, for the Lord, whose name is Jealous, is a jealous God), Lest you make a covenant with the inhabitants of the land, and they play the harlot with their gods and make sacrifice to their gods, and one of them invites you and you eat of his sacrifice, And you take of his daughters for your sons, and his daughters play the harlot with their gods and make your sons play the harlot with their gods. (Exodus 34:13–16 NKJV)

> Nor shall you make marriages with them. You shall not give your daughter to their son, nor take their daughter for your son. For they will turn your sons away from following Me, to serve other gods; so, the anger of the Lord will be aroused against you and destroy you suddenly. But thus you shall deal with them: you shall destroy their altars, and break down their sacred pillars, and cut down their wooden images, and burn their carved images with fire. For you are a holy people to the Lord your God; the Lord

your God has chosen you to be a people for Himself,
a special treasure above all the peoples on the face of
the earth. (Deuteronomy 7:3–6 NKJV)

Do not be unequally yoked together with unbelievers.
For what fellowship has righteousness with
lawlessness? And what communion has light with
darkness? And what accord has Christ with Belial?
Or what part has a believer with an unbeliever?
And what agreement has the temple of God with
idols? For you are the temple of the living God.
As God has said: "I will dwell in them and walk
among them. I will be their God, and they shall be
My people. Therefore "Come out from among them
and be separate," says the Lord. Do not touch what
is unclean, And I will receive you." "I will be a Father
to you, and you shall be My sons and daughters, Says
the Lord Almighty." (2 Corinthians 6:14–18 NKJV)

Therefore, having these promises, beloved, let us
cleanse ourselves from all filthiness of the flesh
and spirit, perfecting holiness in the fear of God. (2
Corinthians 7:1 NKJV)

To whom can you compare God? What image can
you find to resemble him? (Isaiah 40:18 NLT)

For as I was walking along, I saw your many shrines.
And one of your altars had this inscription on it: "To
an Unknown God." This God, whom you worship
without knowing, is the one I'm telling you about.
He is the God who made the world and everything
in it. Since he is Lord of heaven and earth, he doesn't
live in man-made temples, And human hands can't

serve his needs—for he has no needs. He himself gives life and breath to everything, and he satisfies every need. (Acts 17:23–25 NLT)

But a time is coming and is already here when the true worshipers will worship the Father in spirit [from the heart, the inner self] and in truth; for the Father seeks such people to be His worshipers. God is spirit [the Source of life, yet invisible to mankind], and those who worship Him must worship in spirit and truth." (John 4:23–24 AMP)

HIS DIVINE PURPOSE

Purpose was displayed from the beginning of creation. When our Creator and Heavenly Father created the earth, He revealed his plan, will, and purpose to us through His word. After He created the man in Genesis 2:7, He placed the man in the Garden of Eden to dress and to keep it. He commanded him, saying, "Of every tree that's in the garden thou may freely eat, but the tree of knowledge of both good and evil thou shall not eat thereof, for in the day you choose to eat thereof you shall surely die."

After a while, the Father said it was not good for man to be alone and would make him a helper. God put Adam to sleep, took a rib from him, and made a wife for him. Our first parents were living in harmony and walking in right relationship with their Maker. In all that time of living in harmony and peace of mind, and walking hand in hand with his wife, Adam failed to communicate the commandment of God to his wife, Eve.

On that unfortunate day, recorded in Genesis 3, Satan used the availability of the serpent to communicate with the woman. The man stood in silence during the entire conversation between his wife and the serpent.

Eventually, the woman's mind was overpowered, and she gave into the temptation by partaking of the forbidden tree. The devil succeeded in the derailing our Heavenly Father's plan, will, and purpose. When Adam also partook of the fruit, he activated the power of death because of his disobedience. Death had been dead because of obedience, but when disobedience came into existence, death received the power to come alive. Adam also transferred his authority over the entire earth, which he received from his Maker, to Satan. The very moment he disobeyed his Maker, there was a shift in the spiritual realm. (Read Luke 4:5–7.)

The Father's plan was derailed, but only for a season. He was not surprised, and from that moment on, according to Genesis 3:15, the Father started His work to bring redemption and reconciliation to His crown creation. From Noah to Abram, from Isaac to Jacob, from Joseph to Moses, from Joshua to Gideon, from Samson to Ruth, from the prophet Samuel to King David, the Father of Spirits has called men and women to represent Him and fulfill His will and their purposes for living through Him. From Elisabeth to Mary, from John the Baptist to Jesus, and from the apostles to us, this continues.

Throughout creation, before the fullness of time for the promised Son, God has called men and women into His service, so His will may become a reality in the minds and hearts of his covenant people. God called Abram out of his father's house so He could start the plan of redemption. Abram obeyed God, and the Father was truly pleased with his response. Abram was promised a lot of goodies. God said He would make Abram a great nation; He would bless him and make his name great, and he would be a blessing. He would bless those who bless Abram and curse those who curse him. In him, all families of the earth would be blessed. What more can a mere human being ask for? Abram became a friend of God because of his obedience and righteousness. After years of being childless, the Lord blessed Abram with his promised seed through his wife Sarah. She gave birth to a son, who he named Isaac. This was the beginning and formation of the promised nation of which Abram was the father.

Isaac grew up and had a family of his own. His wife bore twins, Esau and Jacob. Jacob stole the birthright from his brother and had to flee for his life. He ran to another land and his uncle Laban. Jacob fell in love and had to work fourteen years to obtain his heart's desire: Rachel. Throughout the years of his stay, the Lord blessed Jacob with sons and a daughter and much livestock. Eventually, he left with all his belongings and returned to his own country. All this time, the will of God was unfolding through the promises He made to Abraham and his seed. The Lord caused a famine throughout the earth. This caused Jacob and his entire household to go into Egypt, so they could be preserved and taken care of.

For all that befell Joseph before the famine, being sold into slavery and taken to Egypt was God's divine plan in action. Joseph was sent so the formation of the promised nation would be preserved. It grew over a period of 430 years. No one would be able to number the people, according to God's word.

The Bible said that, at the end of the 430 years, the Lord would bring deliverance to His people through His servant Moses. The people were set free from bondage and slavery. Not many days after, the people began to rebel and murmur against God and His servant Moses. From that time until this very day, God's covenant people have continued to rebel against Him. God has raised up other nations and caused His people to be enslaved for their disobedience. Only a few of them in every generation have vowed in their hearts not to contaminate themselves with the customs, traditions, and religious beliefs of the foreign land into which they were carried by force. The people of the land had their beliefs in gods other than Jehovah, but few Jews purposed to keep the commandments of their God despite the rugged conditions in which they were living.

As we investigate the following paragraphs concerning Ezra, Esther, and Daniel, we will see and understand that there is always a remnant that chooses to remain faithful to their God and His commandments. It doesn't matter where you were born in or if you migrated to another or were carried as a prisoner into a foreign land, as some of the Jewish people. This matters not. It all boils down to *choice.* Time and seasons change, but God's Word remains the same. His core values and principles will never change because He's the same yesterday, today, and forever. He's the Alpha and Omega, the beginning and the end, and the first and the last. He never changes and neither does His word.

■ ■ ■

The return of the Jewish people to their own land came about after the capture of Babylon by the Persian Empire. Unlike the Babylonians, the Persians allowed their captive nations to live in their own native regions under the authority of a ruling governor. The Persians also practiced religious tolerance, allowing each nation to worship their own God or gods. This explains the proclamation of Cyrus of Persia, which allowed the Jewish people to return to Jerusalem and rebuild their temple. Cyrus even returned the temple treasures that the Babylonians took when they destroyed Jerusalem over forty years earlier Ezra 1:7–11.

The book of Ezra is a historical book that describes the resettlement of the Jewish people in their homeland after their long exile in Babylon. Ezra led the exiles in a new commitment to God's law after their return, for he was a scribe and priest. The book contains ten chapters, and is divided into two distinctive parts. Chapters 1 through 6 outline the return of the first wave of exiles to Jerusalem under the leadership of Zerubbabel. Chapters 7 through 10 describe the return of a second group under Ezra's leadership.

There were 49,897 Jews who returned under the leadership of Zerubbabel. He was a Jewish citizen appointed by Cyrus as governor of Jerusalem. After returning to their country, they set out to rebuild the Temple. The work started and moved forward until the Temple was completed, as recorded in Ezra 6:13–15.

Ezra arrived in Jerusalem with another group of exiles about sixty years after the Temple had been completed. As a scribe and priest,

Ezra's mission was to lead his people to rebuild the Law of God in their hearts. He led the returned captives in Jerusalem to make a new commitment to God's Law. Ezra was trained in the knowledge of the Law while living in captivity in Babylon with other citizens of the nation of Judah. Ezra gained favor during the reign of Artaxerxes, king of Persia. This king commissioned him to return to Jerusalem to bring order among the people of the new community. According to Ezra 7:11, Artaxerxes even gave Ezra a royal letter granting him civil as well as religious authority, along with the finances to furnish the Temple, which had been rebuilt by the returned captives.

Ezra was a skilled scribe and teacher with extensive training in the books of the Law. When he arrived in Jerusalem, Ezra discovered that many of the Hebrew men had married foreign wives from the surrounding nations (Ezra 9:1–2). After a period of prayer and fasting, he insisted that these men divorce their wives (Ezra 10). He feared that intermarriage with pagans would lead to worship of pagan gods in the restored community of Judah.

In addition to these marriage reforms, Ezra also led his people to give attention to reading the Law of God. Several priests helped Ezra read, translate, and interpret the Law for the people's clear understanding in their new language, Aramaic. This reading process went on for seven days as the people focused on God's commandments.

The result of this week of concentration on their heritage was a religious revival. The people confessed their sins and renewed their covenant with God (Nehemiah 9–10).

Ezra was devoted to his God and the high standards of holiness and righteousness that the Lord demanded of His people.

As he communicated God's requirements to the captives in Jerusalem, Ezra also proved he was a capable leader who could point out their shortcomings while leading them to a higher commitment to God's Law. Through it all, Ezra worked with a keen sense of divine guidance, according to the good hand of his God upon him (Ezra 7:9).

The Book of Ezra also teaches a valuable lesson about the providence of God. Several different Persian kings are mentioned in this book. Each king played a significant role in returning God's covenant people to their homeland and helping them restore the Temple as the center of their religious life. This shows that God can use pagans as well as believers to work His ultimate will in the lives of His covenant and kingdom people.

■ ■ ■

The story of Esther's rise from an unknown Jewish girl to queen of a mighty empire illustrates how God uses events and people as instruments to fulfill His will and promises to His chosen people. Following several months of revelry and drunkenness, the drunken king Ahasuerus asked his queen, Vashti, to display herself to his guests. When the queen courageously refused, she was banished from the palace. Ahasuerus then had all the beautiful young virgins of his kingdom brought to his palace so he could choose a new queen to replace Vashti.

Scripture records that Esther was lovely and beautiful (Esther 2:7. The king loved Esther more than all the other virgins, and he appointed her queen to replace Vashti.

At the time, Haman was most trusted advisor to King Ahasuerus. He was a very ambitious man. Haman demanded that people bow to him as he passed, something that Mordecai, a devout Jew, could not do in good conscience. In rage, Haman sought revenge not only on Mordecai but also on the entire Jewish population living in the empire. He persuaded the king to issue an order permitting him to execute all the Jews and seize their property. The king never knew that the order he gave to Haman would also terminate Queen Esther, who he truly loved, because she was also a Jew.

With great wisdom and skill, Esther used her royal favor to intervene and expose Haman's plot. Esther exposed Haman's plot and true character to the king. As a result, Ahasuerus granted the Jews the right to defend themselves and destroy their enemies. With ironic justice, they first hanged Haman on the same gallows he had prepared for Mordecai. After that, they captured Haman's sons and hanged them also. Mordecai was promoted by the king, and the Jewish people rejoiced in God for deliverance and preservation of their lives. They also instituted the Feast of Purim to mark their miraculous deliverance.

The Book of Esther is a major chapter in the struggle of God's people to survive in a hostile world. Beginning with the Book of Genesis, God made it clear that he would bless His covenant people and bring a curse upon those who tried to do them harm. This was according to the promise He made to Abram (Genesis 12:1–3). The Book of Esther also shows how God has kept this promise at every stage of history. Shortly after the Persians overthrew the Babylonians, they allowed the Jewish exiles to return to their native land. Many returned to Jerusalem, but thousands of Jewish citizens chose to remain in Persia for whatever reason. Probably, it had become home for them during their long separation from their native land.

The book shows clearly that God protects His chosen people, even when they are scattered among the nations of the world.

One unusual fact about this book is that it never mentions the name of God. The book also teaches us a valuable lesson about the sovereignty of Jehovah. Although the enemies of the covenant people may triumph for a season, He holds the key to ultimate victory.

■　■　■

Daniel was a teenager when he was taken from Jerusalem into captivity by the Babylonians along with his three friends, Hananiah, Mishael, and Azariah. They were taken captive in one of the Babylonian raids against Judah. They were all intelligent and fervent in the things of God. Despite their situations over the years, their walks with God grew from strength to strength. They were totally focused on their commitments toward God. They were placed in special training as servants in the court of King Nebuchadnezzar. Their names and diets were changed to reflect Babylonian culture and to take away their Jewish identity and nature. However, Daniel and his friends rose to the challenge, proving their Jewish food was superior to the diet of the Babylonians. The young men increased in wisdom and knowledge, gaining favor in the king's court.

Daniel wasn't just a prophet because of the prophetic dimensions of the book. He also served as an advisor in the courts of foreign kings. Daniel remained in governmental service through the reigns of the kings of Babylon and into the reign of Cyrus of Persia after the Persians became the dominant world power (Daniel 1:19–21; 10:1). Daniel was also a person of deep piety. From his youth, Daniel was determined to live by God's law in a distant land (Daniel 1:5–9). In moments of crisis, Daniel turned first to God in prayer before turning to the affairs of state (Daniel 2:14–23).

Daniel and his friends underwent several additional tests to prove that although they were being held captive by a pagan people, the God they worshiped was still in control. Daniel's three friends were renamed Shadrach, Meshach, and Abednego. They refused to worship the pagan Babylonian gods. They were eventually cast into the fiery furnace. However, God was with them even there, and they emerged unharmed because of God's miraculous protection.

His enemies even used his regular prayer life to trap him and turn the king against him. However, the grace and uncommon favor of God protected Daniel, as described in chapter 6. Daniel (whose name means "God is my judge") was rescued miraculously from a den of hungry lions after he refused to bow down and worship a pagan king. These tests proved that the God they served was superior to the pagan gods of their captors. Daniel wrote to show that God was and is still in control of world history, and that He had not yet finished with His covenant people.

■ ■ ■

God's covenant people were carried away as captives into slavery. Some choose to remain faithful to their God and His commandments; they refused to contaminate themselves with their surroundings. They remembered His goodness toward them despite their conditions. They understood that their nation's rebellion and disobedience toward Him caused them all to be carried into slavery.

Many of you were involved in ministry back in your countries. Some of you were even pastors of ministries. You were on fire for God and involved in everything in the church. You decided to leave your countries and travel to a foreign land to continue in ministry. You said the Holy Spirit was leading you to go, and He had already started to open doors. You made the necessary preparations which are required of you as the pastors of your churches. You passed the batons to other faithful people you trusted. You said farewell to the congregations, as the apostle Paul did in Acts 20:17–38.

Both ministers and lay members of different congregations throughout the world have left their respective countries. They have said they were going to do the Lord's work in the United States. Many of them, after landing at JFK International Airport, eventually laid down their callings, passions, and desires for God and His work on the altar of compromise for milk and honey, as the saying goes. Some of us have entered these foreign lands through the leading of the Holy Spirit. We strive purposefully, filled with visions and on fire for the kingdom of God and Jesus Christ. Many have derailed from their true purposes and relationships with God. They became caught up in the wind of success and prosperity. Eventually the winds of rebellion, disobedience, immorality, unrighteousness, and sin took over.

Church services were scheduled three times a week. You were involved in every service because you were on fire for God. You managed your time properly so you would be in God's house when you ought to be there. After a time, your involvement in the services decreased. Your fire and desire for the things of God wasn't there anymore. Eventually, you ended attending one service each week on Sunday morning. You became a Sunday morning church attendee. Eventually, you just slipped away from fellowship without any conviction whatsoever. You were caught up with the cares of this world, just as Jesus described in Mark 4:19 (AMP)

> But the worries and cares of the world [the distractions of this age with its worldly pleasures], and the deceitfulness [and the false security or glamour] of wealth [or fame], and the passionate desires for all the other things creep in and choke out the word, and it becomes unfruitful.

The word of God is truth, and it reveals the end from the beginning. Even so, men and women are so ignorant, they give it all away for false glamour and worldly security. They fail to realize that eternity is a long time to spend in the wrong place.

However, there's a clarion call to come back home. It is a call for all who rebelled and disobeyed Jehovah God to return to their true source. It is a call to repentance, a call to revival, and a call to fulfill original visions and purposes in God.

People become true leaders when they make the decision not to sacrifice their principles and core values on the altar of convenience and compromise. Life is not about what you want to do; it's about what must be done. Until you change your ideas and mindset, you will never change your life. It was easier for God to deliver the children of Israel from the hands of Pharaoh than to change their minds or the way they thought. It's all up to you. What do you consider important? Is it your job, your friends, or your big house? Is it your family and where all of you will spend eternity? True leaders pass the batons on before they die, and they live to see the other people run their courses in excellence, passion, and fire for God.

Scriptures for Your Reading and Admonition

> You, therefore, my son, be strong in the grace that is in Christ Jesus. And the things that you have heard from me among many witnesses, commit these to faithful men who will be able to teach others also. You therefore must endure hardship as a good soldier of Jesus Christ. No one engaged in warfare entangles himself with the affairs of this life, that he may please him who enlisted him as a soldier. And also if anyone competes in athletics, he is not crowned unless he competes according to the rules. (2 Timothy 2:1–5 NKJV)

> Declaring the end and the result from the beginning, and from ancient times the things which have not [yet] been done, Saying, "My purpose will be established, And I will do all that pleases Me and fulfills My purpose." (Isaiah 46:10 AMP)

> You can make many plans, but the LORD's purpose will prevail. (Proverbs 19:21 NLT)

> Declare and present your defense of idols; indeed, let them consult together. Who announced this [rise of Cyrus and his conquests] long before it happened? Who declared it long ago? Was it not I, the LORD? And there is no other God besides Me, A [consistently and uncompromisingly]

just and righteous God and a Savior; there is none except Me. (Isaiah 45:21 AMP)

There is no [human] wisdom or understanding or counsel [that can prevail] against the LORD. (Proverbs 21:30 AMP)

Then the captain went with the officers and brought them without violence, for they feared the people, lest they should be stoned. And when they had brought them, they set them before the council. And the high priest asked them. Saying, "Did we not strictly command you not to teach in this name? And look, you have filled Jerusalem with your doctrine, and intend to bring this Man's blood on us!" But Peter and the other apostles answered and said: "We ought to obey God rather than men. The God of our fathers raised up Jesus whom you murdered by hanging on a tree. Him God has exalted to His right hand to be Prince and Savior, to give repentance to Israel and forgiveness of sins. And we are His witnesses to these things, and so also is the Holy Spirit whom God has given to those who obey Him." When they heard this, they were furious and plotted to kill them. Then one in the council stood up, a Pharisee named Gamaliel, a teacher of the law held in respect by all the people and commanded them to put the apostles outside for a little while. And he said to them: "Men of Israel, take heed to yourselves what you intend to do regarding these men. For some time ago Theurosee rose up, claiming to be somebody. A number of men, about four hundred, joined him. He was slain, and all who obeyed him were scattered and came to nothing. After this man, Judas of Galilee rose up in the days of census and drew away many people after him. He also perished, and all who obeyed him were dispersed. And now I say to you, keep away from these men and let them alone; for if this plan or this work is of men, it will come to nothing. But if it is of God, you cannot overthrow it—lest you even be found to fight against God." And they agreed with him, and when they had called for the apostles and beaten them, they commanded that they should not speak in the name of Jesus and let them go. So they departed from the presence of the council, rejoicing that they were counted worthy to suffer shame for His name. And daily in the temple, and in every house, they did not cease teaching and preaching Jesus as the Christ. (Acts 5:26–42 NKJV)

May God our Father and the Lord Jesus Christ give you grace and peace. All praise to God, the Father of our Lord Jesus Christ, who has blessed us with every spiritual blessing in the heavenly realms because we are united with Christ. Even before he made the world, God loved us and chose us in Christ to be holy and without fault in his eyes. God decided in advance to adopt us into his own family by bringing us to himself through Jesus Christ. This is what he wanted to do, and it gave him great pleasure. So we praise God for the glorious grace he has poured out on us who belong to his dear Son. He is so rich in kindness and grace that he purchased our freedom with the blood of his Son and forgave our sins. He has showered his kindness on us, along with all wisdom and understanding. God has now revealed to us his mysterious will regarding Christ—which is to fulfill his own good plan. And this is the plan: At the right time he will bring everything together under the authority of Christ—everything in heaven and on earth. Furthermore, because we are united with Christ, we have received an inheritance from God for he chose us in advance, and he makes everything work out according to his plan. (Ephesians 1:2–11 NLT)

There is a way which seems right to a man and appears straight before him, but its end is the way of death. (Proverbs 14:12 AMP)

Enter through the narrow gate. For wide is the gate and broad and easy to travel is the path that leads the way to destruction and eternal loss, and there are many who enter through it. But small is the gate and narrow and difficult to travel is the path that leads the way to [everlasting] life, and there are few who find it. (Matthew 7:13–14 AMP)

Understand this, my dear brothers, and sisters: You must all be quick to listen, slow to speak, and slow to get angry. Human anger does not produce the righteousness God desires. So get rid of all the filth and evil in your lives, and humbly accept the word God has planted in your hearts, for it has the power to save your souls. But don't just listen to God's word. You must do what it says. Otherwise, you are only fooling yourselves. For if you listen to the word and don't obey, it is like glancing at your face in a mirror. You see yourself, walk away, and forget what you look like. But if you look carefully into the perfect law that sets you free, and if you do what it says and don't forget what you heard, then God will bless you for doing it. (James 1:19–25 NLT)

FOR ME, TO LIVE IS CHRIST

This is a true-life event of two wonderful individuals: Zechariah (whose name means "the Lord has remembered") and Elizabeth (whose name means "God is my oath"). Zechariah was a priest of the division of Abijah. His wife was one of the daughters of Aaron, meaning she also came out of a priestly line. That is very important to remember. Priests were very careful to marry within their own clans to maintain the dignity of the priesthood and keep it without mixture. They were both righteous before God, and careful to obey all—not some, but all—of the Lord's commandments and ordinances. They were blameless and perfect before Him. They were both approved by God and were accepted. It is a good thing when those who are joined to each other in marriage and are also joined to the Lord in His service.

The Lord commands His ministers to be righteous before Him so they may be examples to the flock and rejoice in their hearts. Zechariah and Elizabeth were at peace with themselves and with their commitments and devotions in the service of the Lord. Though they were not sinless, they were blameless. No one could have charged or accused them of any wrongdoing or misbehavior in the Lord's service and in their personal lives. They lived honestly as ministers and walked in fear of the Lord. They treated the people in the same manner the Lord treated them. They did not want to bring reproach to the name of their God in whom they both believed and trusted.

Zechariah and his wife had a very serious medical problem that not even doctors could have solved. They had no child and were as old as Abraham and Sarah. Elizabeth was barren. When you understand the marriage customs of the Jewish people, you will realize that Zechariah and Elizabeth married when they were young, probably between the ages of fourteen and twenty-one.

For over fifty years, they tried again and again for a child but there was no conception. They trusted in their eternal source and Maker of all things, yet still had no child. I am sure they even went into a time of prayer and fasting, and still had no child. There was no answer for over fifty years, yet they both remained faithful to God and to their calling. They did not blame each other for their demise, and they surely did not blame God for their childlessness. Their love and faithfulness toward each other were unquestionable. They did not give up on God and He surely did not give up on them either.

I want you to always remember this. The Lord has always set aside a day and a time in which He intervenes on our behalf, because our time is surely not His. The Father knows best. He always brings it at the best-appointed time when it's most needed. When you cannot trace His hands, you must always trust His heart.

On a specific day, Zechariah was serving as priest before God in the order of his division, according to the custom of the priesthood. On that day, through the casting of lots, it fell on him to burn incense in the temple of the Lord. Zechariah entered the Most Holy Place to perform his duties.

While Zechariah was performing his duties without any concern, the only thing probably on his mind was to do everything correctly. To his surprise, there was someone standing at his side. I believe he was saying in his mind, *This cannot be, for no one else is allowed inside of here while I am here.* Fear came upon him. The angel of the Lord spoke to him and encouraged him not to be afraid.

(Then the angel called him by name, Zechariah, I am paraphrasing, yes mister angel, your prayer has been heard, my prayer, which one of them? Your wife Elizabeth will conceive and bear you a son, and you shall call his name John. Are you sure you have come to the right person? Look at my condition and my wife are not any different to me, we are both very old and stricken in years. There are another Zechariah twelve blocks down the road, and he is way younger than me because I taught him in (children's educational hour). He also has a very beautiful wife but am not sure of her age, it could be them).

There are times when we behave like Zechariah when we least expect anything to come our way. So many years passed while we prayed for a specific thing. Suddenly, when the Father sends His messenger with a word, it's hard to believe it after all that time.

Luke 1:5–20 (NLT) says,

> When Herod was king of Judea, there was a Jewish priest named Zechariah. He was a member of the priestly order of Abijah, and his wife, Elizabeth, was also from the priestly line of Aaron. Zechariah and Elizabeth were righteous in God's eyes, careful to obey all of the Lord's commandments and regulations. They had no children because Elizabeth was unable to conceive, and they were both very old. One day Zechariah was serving God in the Temple, for his order was on duty that week. As was the custom of the priests, he was chosen by lot to enter the sanctuary of the Lord and burn incense. While the incense was being burned, a great crowd stood outside, praying. While Zechariah was in the sanctuary, an angel of the Lord appeared to him, standing to the right of the incense altar. Zechariah

was shaken and overwhelmed with fear when he saw him. But the angel said, "Don't be afraid, Zechariah! God has heard your prayer. Your wife, Elizabeth, will give you a son, and you are to name him John. You will have great joy and gladness, and many will rejoice at his birth, for he will be great in the eyes of the Lord. He must never touch wine or other alcoholic drinks. He will be filled with the Holy Spirit, even before his birth. And he will turn many Israelites to the Lord their God. He will be a man with the spirit and power of Elijah. He will prepare the people for the coming of the Lord. He will turn the hearts of the fathers to their children, and he will cause those who are rebellious to accept the wisdom of the godly. Zechariah said to the angel, "How can I be sure this will happen? I'm an old man now, and my wife is also well along in years." Then the angel said, "I am Gabriel! I stand in the very presence of God. It was he who sent me to bring you this good news! But now, since you didn't believe what I said, you will be silent and unable to speak until the child is born. For my words will certainly be fulfilled at the proper time.

Imagine you were a young man with a very beautiful wife. You had money put aside in the bank. You were patiently waiting for your wife to conceive so you could become wonderful parents and bring up your child in the ways of the Lord. You had been trusting in the Lord for years for this one request, still being faithful to Him and the things which pertain to the kingdom of God. Your calling, passion, and fire for God were still intact without any wavering, and still there was no child. God has always come through for you from the minute you accepted Jesus as Lord. Every prayer request you made of Him, He brought it to pass in your life—except this one, for a child.

I want you to know and always remember that God knows best, and His time is the best time. Remember that Sarai, Rebekah, Rachel (Samson's mother), and Hannah were barren, but God blessed their wombs and they conceived at the appointed time. They all gave birth to boys.

The most wonderful thing about these women and their children is that they all were used in God's plan of redemption. Sarai gave birth to Isaac. Rebekah was Isaac's wife, and she gave birth to Esau and Jacob. Jacob became the father to the heads of the twelve tribes of Israel. Rachel was Jacob's wife, and she gave birth to Joseph, who was used by God in Egypt to be the preserver of life during the famine.

Samson's mother's name is not mentioned in scripture. He was used to deliver his people Israel from the Philistines. However, he was disobedient to God and his mother, and fell in love with a pagan woman.

Hannah gave birth to Samuel. He grew up in the Lord's house with Eli the priest. God raised him up as a prophet and priest to His people, because the priesthood was corrupt.

For thousands of years, men and women have offered prayers to God and trusted Him to come through for them. They have received answers to some of their petitions right away. Eventually, they died without receiving answers to all their petitions.

Let me ask you a serious question. If you trust God for something and you have already prayed about it (healing, deliverance, or something else) and it does not happen when you expected it to happen, will you turn your back on God? I said before and let me say it again: our time and God's time are totally different and opposite to each other. The Father knows best, and He knows all things. He will come through for you when the time is right. Hold on. Weeping may endure but for a night, but joy comes in the morning. *Just stand still and see the salvation of your God.*

■ ■ ■

As a young man growing up in the Caribbean, life was very good but difficult at times, just like everywhere else in the world. Trinidad in the years of my youth was great. I loved climbing trees, because there are many fruit trees to eat from. There was ground provision to harvest and it was all free. You could have driven up to Heights of Guan-apo Road, which leads to the mountain. Yams grow on their own there with no one to claim them. You could harvest them and put down a good pot of ground provision and saltfish. In those days, I did not know the Lord Jesus or His expectations for my life. However, I knew I was different from my peers. I did not involve myself in violence or trouble. I was involved in sports and smoked lots of marijuana, but I had control over it.

The community I grew up in that was infested with marijuana and cocaine. I knew that if I could not control my marijuana smoking, then I had to stop smoking. Otherwise, I would have ended up taking stronger drugs like cocaine. I said to Nobe, a good friend, "There is more to life than what we are doing at the moment." My desire to control my smoking was greater than my desire to smoke. I refused to become like those who have become hooked on cocaine, and then ended up on the streets and homeless. This is where the devil desires to have humanity. I chose to be different.

I had many near-death experiences in my teenage years. I climbed many trees, and branches have broken while I was on them. I came down flat, at times on my back. At one time, there was a mango tree on our property, and the mangoes were starting to ripen. After climbing the tree and stretching to pick one, I heard the branch crack. After opening my eyes, I was in my father's vehicle returning from the hospital.

It has been forty-three years since that incident happened. I still can't remember anything that happened between hearing the cracks and coming home from the hospital. I could have died without knowing how it felt to have a family of my own, a wife and children. I realized I had landed on my left side when I hit the ground. I did not know the Lord at that time, but God's will and mercy kept me.

Worst of it all, I have been in a vehicular accident. The vehicle I was driving went right off the road. It was totaled after I hit three other vehicles. Hitting the vehicles at the speed I was driving propelled me into the air. The vehicle flipped. I ended up in the back seat of the car because I was not using a seat belt at the time. When the car landed and settled, the wheels were facing the sky. One tire and rim was completely missing.

I crawled out from the back seat without any major injuries. I had a scratch and a bump on my forehead. People came looking for the driver and could not believe I was standing outside of the vehicle. The condition of the vehicle meant that I should have died. That I did not was only because of the will and mercy of God upon my life. Hear me clearly: all this time I did not know the Lord. I would have burst hell wide open. However, the Father knew me and the genuineness of my heart, even when I was living in sin and arrogance.

When the Father of all spirits has a special work for you to do, and you have not yet come into the knowledge of the saving grace of God in Christ Jesus, He protects you, without you having the slightest idea of what is going on in the spiritual realm. The apostle Paul writes in Acts 9 that he was once Saul and a persecutor of the early church. On his way to Damascus to arrest the brethren, the Lord Jesus appeared unto him. That encounter changed his life forever into a positive way. His passion for persecuting the church changed into a passion for spreading the truth of the Kingdom of God. The hatred and contempt for the brethren changed to love and prayer for the brethren.

On August 22, 1991, I stopped running, and accepted the Lord Jesus into my heart. It's the best decision that I have ever made in my life. I started a new chapter in my life and started living the life of a true born-again Christian. The Lord has been gracious and merciful to my household and me. On October 5, 1991, I married my friend, my lover, and the mother of my first child. We both gave our hearts to the Lord on that same night in August.

God is so merciful to us. He sent His people from Word Revival Ministry to keep a crusade next door to me at the house of my neighbor, Miss Dou. On the second night of the service, we gave our hearts to the Lord.

We started attending church services. Weekly, we fellowshipped with the brethren in the presence of the Lord. The first Bible I purchased was an amplified Bible, and I started studying it. Every week, we would have street meetings and give out tracts. Before the passing of the pastor's wife, Sister Rebecca, the Lord used her mightily for a few months. Sunday after Sunday, the service would last about five hours. Even when the service was over, the people did not want to go home. I miss those days. One Sunday service, we had a visiting preacher, a prophet of God called Vernon Duncan. He prophesied over our lives and told us the Lord said we would be in a foreign land teaching the Word of God. It took thirteen and a half years for it to come to pass. On March 16, 2005, the Lord brought me to the United States of America, and my wife came in December of that same year.

My greatest passion then and now is the passion for knowing the truth about the contents of the Bible. I study the scriptures so I can understand the only true God and His requirements for my life, my family, and His people. Then, I will be able teach the truth of His word. We can then apply it to every aspect of our lives and choose to do what pleases Him.

Knowing and obeying scripture are the twin foundations of a godly life. A godly life produces the further desire to study God's Word. Bible interpretation done properly takes the student from study to application back to study and on to further application in a mounting spiral toward God. Satan attempts to take away our desire to study scripture. This is nothing less than an attempt to remove the basis of our spiritual growth and stability. That is why over hundreds of years, Satan has succeeded in derailing millions in the church, keeping them occupied and focused on things other than those that bring spiritual growth and stability in one's life.

However, it is essential to recognize that the principal purpose of Biblical teaching is to preserve truth and to produce holiness in God's people by leading Christ's body into an uncompromising commitment to the godly lifestyle set forth in God's Word. Study is not complete until we put into practice what we have learned. The question to ask at this stage of interpretation is how I can apply what I have learned to how I live my life.

As the Apostle Paul said in Philippians 3:12–14 (NKJV),

> Not that I have already attained, or am already perfected; but I press on, that I may lay hold of that for which Christ Jesus has also laid hold of me. Brethren, I do not count myself to have apprehended; but one thing I do, forgetting those things which are behind and reaching forward to those things which are ahead. I press toward the goal for the prize of the upward call of God in Christ Jesus.

My past is the foundation for my future,
and I choose not to visit my past.

My wife and I started fellowshipping in Queens, New York and started working with a few pastors. My wife is a worship leader, and I am a teacher of the scriptures with the heart of a shepherd. After one Sunday service, a brother gave us a lift to our home. He asked, "Pastor Peter, since you have been at the ministry, what have you learnt?"

I will not mention the name of the church or churches we have worked with, but my answer to him was this: "I have learnt what not to do." He laughed. For some reason, I believe we were considered a threat to a lot of these pastors. I believe this was because of the way we chose to be different and how we treated God's people with respect and love. All we wanted to do was be a blessing to the ministry and the people, for that's how we understand it through the Word of God. On an old year's night service in 2012, the Spirit of God spoke to me while I was worshipping. He gave me the name of the ministry that we would have to register to start the work for which He brought me to the United States. The name of the ministry is Word of Reconciliation. He spoke to me again about 2:30 a.m. New Year's morning and gave me the vision for the ministry: *reconciling men and women from every culture and nation through the teaching of the Word and the power of the Gospel of Jesus Christ.*

On one Saturday morning, we had a leaders' meeting. The senior pastor said to the assistant pastor, to get support from him, "Reverend, the messages that Pastor Peter is teaching to the people, he's the one who supposed to be teaching them that, because he's the senior pastor". I was surprised to hear this big boy behaving like that. Everybody has a Bible. I did not have a special one. He could preach whatever he wanted to because he's the senior pastor. The things I have seen and heard in that ministry and other ministries are unbelievable.

I have seen spiritual manipulation in a big way. I have seen money manipulation. I witnessed visiting preachers prophesying lies. The senior pastor allowed it to continue, but protected his wife and children by sending them home with one of the brethren. Sometimes when the senior pastor was not around, a visiting preacher came to minister. Afterward, the IT department were already instructed to play the senior pastor's prayer CD so the people would know to trust in his voice for healing and deliverance even if he was not there. We eventually left that ministry and went to help another pastor.

The Lord directed us to go to upstate New York to carry on His work. We were waiting on God for direction on purchasing a building for ministry. While we were waiting, we fellowshipped at Agape Apostolic Church in Troy, New York. Week after week, from the very first time we visited, we have heard nothing less but the truth of the Word, for they are sound in the Word of God and His doctrine.

Minister Justin, Pastor Shalako, and the worship team lead the live worship. They are truly amazing, for they are a loving and caring bunch of individuals. Senior Pastor Camp and his beautiful wife Evangelist Paulette are truly a humble and selfless pair of godly servants. In all the ministries we have worked along with in the Queens, New York area, we truly have not come across such a pair of selfless leaders who love the Lord and the people of God.

They make time for you, time to pray for you and your family, or time to visit you in the hospital if ever it reaches that point. If there's a need, they will address it.

Every month, they provide food and sometimes clothing and shoes for over three hundred families through their Bread of Life Food Pantry. It is led by Minister Anthony. They are a bunch of brethren who love the Lord Jesus. Love is the highest quality that enables a true leader to sacrificially give to others.

My wife and I are truly honored and grateful to God that we are there in this season while we wait on the Father for direction. We are there to be a blessing to the ministry and the people. Wherever we can help, we help. Even after we leave to continue with the work the Lord has brought us to this country to do, we will still be part of that family of believers and continue to be a blessing. *You can't outgive God at any time.* This is for the glory of the Father and the furtherance of the gospel of Jesus Christ. It's the best way to give back from what was entrusted to us in the first place. We cannot leave everything for future generations. We are doing this for them so God will bless and keep them after we depart from the earth. When we die, we can't carry anything with us.

Recently, Elder Mackey ministered on a Bible study night. He said he had never seen a U-Haul following a hearse. Naked you come and naked you shall return, saith the Lord. I can truly say I have learned what to do. Amen. I will leave you with this verse of scripture. My wife and I do what we do because of this verse. Paul said in 1 Corinthians 15:58 (AMP),

Therefore, my beloved brothers and sisters, be steadfast, immovable, always excelling in the work of the Lord [always doing your best and doing more than is needed], being continually aware that your labor [even to the point of exhaustion] in the Lord is not futile nor wasted [it is never without purpose].

Jesus said in John 10:11–15 (AMP),

I am the Good Shepherd. The Good Shepherd lays down His [own] life for the sheep. But the hired man [who merely serves for wages, who is neither the shepherd nor the owner of the sheep, when he sees the wolf coming, deserts the flock and runs away; and the wolf snatches the sheep and scatters them. The man runs because he is a hired hand [who serves only for wages] and is not concerned about the [safety of the sheep]. I am the Good Shepherd, and I know [without any doubt those who are] My own and my own know Me [and have a deep, personal relationship with Me]. Even as the Father knows Me, and I know the Father—and I lay down My [very own] life [sacrificing it] for the benefit of the sheep.

As believers in Christ Jesus and as we walk and live the lives laid out for us in scriptures, we must realize that it's most important to secure our individual destinies before death comes our way or the rapture of the church occurs. We must not put our souls in the hands of the person or people we are sitting under. It is too important to lose. We must be able to protect those who are closest to us, namely, our families. That's why it is important to study the scriptures for ourselves. We must not be lazy or too busy, otherwise we will lose it all. We must study, and study, and then apply the Word to our lives. We must ask the Holy Spirit to teach us and reveal the truths of the

Word to us. Then we can truly be kings and priests in our homes, and leaders in our places of employment.

As the king, you have a responsibility to provide the necessities for your family and to protect them. As the priest, it is your solemn duty to minister to your family at home first and decide the best direction for your family spiritually speaking. There are too many imposters standing behind the pulpits. Yes, you must fellowship because the scriptures said so, but you must observe your surroundings. Most important, you must understand what is being said from behind the pulpit. Do not lose focus on what is being said.

As Dr. Nassir Sidiki said, "Wherever you are, be there." This means if you are in church, let your mind be in church also, not in the grocery or on your job. He also said, "Faith comes by hearing, it stays by understanding and the spirit man grows by application."

Live out the Word of God in your daily walk.

In 1 John 2:24–29 (NLT), we read,

> So you must remain faithful to what you have been taught from the beginning. If you do, you will remain in fellowship with the Son and with the Father. And in this fellowship, we enjoy the eternal life he promised us. I am writing these things to warn you about those who want to lead you astray. But you have received the Holy Spirit, and he lives within you, so you don't need anyone to teach you what is true. For the Spirit teaches you everything you need to know, and what he teaches is true—it is not a lie. So just as he has taught you, remain in fellowship with Christ. And now, dear children, remain in fellowship with Christ so that when he returns, you will be full of courage and not shrink back from him in shame. Since we know that Christ

is righteous, we also know that all who do what is right are God's children.

As people who profess love for God, we must be very careful not to allow envy and jealousy to enter our hearts. We must never come to the place where we compare gifts given to us for the sole purpose of the ministry, the people, and the Kingdom of God. We are threatened over each others' callings. We assume the other people are more anointed because they are operating in the gifts of miracles, signs, and wonders. We must understand that *grace* can carry us to heaven without the working of miracles. However, the working of *miracles* cannot carry us to heaven without grace. If we want to operate in the gifts of the Holy Spirit, nothing is wrong with that because we desire something great.

My question to you is whether you are willing to pay the price. This does not mean money. Are you willing to make the necessary sacrifices by denying yourself, spending time in prayer and fasting, frequently changing your mindset, and not being selfish and greedy for monetary gains?

The late Samuel Dyer said in his song "Loving Arms," "They say I'm anointed, holy, I don't want to preach about miracles, and then You say that You don't know me."[1]

John said in Revelation 22:10–16 (NLT),

> Then he instructed me, "Do not seal up the prophetic words in this book, for the time is near. Let the one who is doing harm continue to do harm; let the one who is vile continue to be vile; let the one who is righteous, continue to live righteously; let the one who is holy continue to be holy." "Look, I am coming soon, bringing my reward with me to repay all people according to their deeds. I am the Alpha and the

[1] Samuel Dyer, "Loving Arms," Dyers Promotions, September 9, 2011, YouTube video, 5:12, https://www.youtube.com/watch?v=ngyTBMWLqvI.

Omega, the First and the Last, the Beginning and the End." Blessed are those who wash their robes. They will be permitted to enter through the gates of the city and eat the fruit from the tree of life. Outside the city are the dogs—the sorcerers, the sexually immoral, the murderers, the idol worshipers, and all who love to live a lie. "I, Jesus, have sent my angel to give you this message for the churches. I am both the source of David and the heir to his throne. I am the bright morning star."

I have seen and heard about things that happened in churches while ministering here in New York. These are things I have not experienced or heard of in my country while I was still there. At times, right after service is over, you see the brethren come outside and immediately light up tobacco sticks. They were uneasy while service was still active. According to the late R.W Schambach, they had a tobacco fits while in service. That was a big surprise to me.

My wife and I were in a service one Sunday evening. When they picked up the offering, the pastor told them to count it. The offering was not enough, so they were instructed to pick up another offering. May God have mercy upon the church. Then again, tares and wheat must grow together. Pastors use the brothers as shields to protect them from the dangers that may come their way. Isn't it written that the shepherd is supposed to protect the sheep? Some things said to me regarding what some families underwent in some ministries are unbelievable. Imagine that you must ask your pastor when you can have sex with your spouse.

My wife has a friend from when she used to take vocal lessons. The friend' daughter lives in Philadelphia who attends a particular church. She told her mother that the pastor's son is having sex with the women in the church and nothing is being done about it. She eventually left, but this reminds me of Eli and his two sons. After a while, God's judgment came upon them. Some pastors behave like they own you. They don't want you making any plans unless you consult with them and get their approval. These imposters need to be saved. They truly need Jesus. This type of behavior is devilish and not of God.

The Bible said in 1 Peter 5:1–4 (AMP),

> Therefore, I strongly urge the elders among you [pastors, spiritual leaders of the church], as a fellow elder and as an eyewitness [called to testify] of the sufferings of Christ, as well as one who shares in the glory that is to be revealed. Shepherd and guide and protect the flock of God among you, exercising oversight not under compulsion, but voluntarily, according to the will of God; and not [motivated] for shameful gain, but with wholehearted enthusiasm. Not lording it over those assigned to your care [do not be arrogant or overbearing] but be examples [of Christian living] to the flock [set a pattern of integrity for your congregation]. And when the Chief Shepherd (Christ) appears, you will receive the [conqueror's] unfading crown of glory.

Do you see the principles and integrity an elder is supposed to live by? We ought to abide according to the guidelines of the scriptures. It seems that they themselves don't know the scriptures. According to Hebrews 6, while they ought to be teachers, they need someone to teach them all over again. That's why before I started ministry, I studied the life of a shepherd, the one who takes care of the sheep—I am talking about the animals themselves. I learned how shepherds sometimes put themselves in danger to protect the animals because of the love and care they have for the sheep. That is why the greatest individuals who ever led God's people in the Old Testament were Moses and David. They were shepherds before God called them to lead His people. They understood the life and nature of the animal.

They had hearts for what they were doing before God called them to lead.

We must come to the place of understanding when we are called into ministry. However, few are called into *office*. Being called into *office* is all about your heart condition. You must have a heart to serve, to lead by example, to love, to protect, to stand in the gap for the people, to feed and nourish, and to give back to the people when there's a financial need. You must be accessible to all not just a few because of anticipated monetary gains. You must respect all and not just a few. You must make time to see everyone, even though there will be a few miserable ones in the midst. I could go on with this, but I believe and hope that you got it.

Do not be like King Rehoboam in 1 Kings 12:1–19. He had yes men around him who were only seeking favor. Keep leaders around you who will keep you safe. When you do wrong, they are not afraid to let you know that you have erred.

Jesus said He is the good shepherd, and He lays down His life for the sheep. Let us live by the examples, principles, and integrity of our Master, Jesus. Paul also said to follow him as he has followed Christ. Paul said in Philippians 1, "For me to live is Christ." In other words, regardless of what evil befell him, he would continue to live his life for Jesus to the end. His life revolved around Jesus and the finished work on the cross.

We must strive to be holy, for without holiness, no person shall see God. We must also work toward excellence and perfection in the way we live and in the service of the Lord.

I love to study the scriptures not just read them. When I came across this portion of scriptures, it blew my mind. Our existence in Christ Jesus is tied into this portion of scripture in Genesis 17:1–2 (AMP).

When Abram was ninety-nine years old, the LORD appeared to him and said, "I am God Almighty; walk [habitually] before Me [with integrity, knowing that you are always in My presence], and be blameless and complete [in obedience to Me]. "I will establish My covenant (everlasting promise) between Me and you, And I will multiply you exceedingly [through your descendants]."

Deuteronomy 10:12–13 (AMP) says,

And now, Israel, what does the LORD your God require from you, but to fear [and worship] the LORD your God [with awe-filled reverence and profound respect], to walk [that is, to live each and every day] in all His ways and to love Him, and to serve the LORD your God with all your heart and with all your soul [your choices, your thoughts, your whole being]. And to keep the commandments of the LORD and His statutes which I am commanding you today for your good?

Here is a most pathetic exhortation to obedience, Moses brings it in like an orator with an appeal to his audience when he says, "And now, Israel, what doth the Lord thy God require of thee?" (Deuteronomy 10:12).You must ask what He requires. As David says in Psalm 116:12, "What shall I render unto the Lord for all his benefits?" When we have received mercy from God, we should ask what returns we shall make to Him, because we cannot take His mercies for granted.

Consider what he requires and you will find it is nothing but what is highly just, reasonable and of unspeakable benefit. It's an advantage to you. Let us see here what he does require, and what abundant reasons there are why we should do what he requires.

We are directed in our duty to God, to our neighbor, and to ourselves. We are taught our duty to God, both in the dispositions and affections of our souls and in the actions of our lives, our principles, and our practices.

We must fear the Lord our God. We must adore His majesty, acknowledge His authority, stand in awe of His power, and dread His wrath.

We must love Him and be well pleased that He is who He said He is. We must desire that He may be ours, delight in the contemplation of Him, and be in communion with Him. We must fear Him, for He is the God of all flesh and our Lord. We must love Him for He has been good to us. He's our Father and benefactor.

We must walk in all of his ways, which he has appointed for us to walk in. The whole course of our conversation must be conformable to His holy will. We must serve Him with all our hearts and souls, devote ourselves to His honor, and choose to advance all the interests of His kingdom among people. We must be hearty and zealous in His service. We must engage and employ our entire beings, bodies, souls, and spirits in His work. What we do for Him we must do cheerfully and with a good will.

We must keep His commandments and His statutes. Having given ourselves up to His service, we must make His revealed will our rule in everything. We must do all He prescribes, forbear all the forbidden, and firmly believe that all the statutes he commands are for our own good.

Besides the reward of obedience, which will be our unspeakable gain, there is true honor and pleasure in obedience. It is really for our present good to be meek and humble, chaste, sober, just, charitable, patient, and contented. These make us easy, safe, pleasant, and truly great.

To Him we must cleave, having chosen Him for our God. We must faithfully and constantly abide with Him and never forsake Him. He is the one we love and ought to delight, trust, and confide in, and from whom we have great expectations and an eternal hope.

As a teacher of the scriptures, I choose to live by example, because I cannot demand from the people what I do not possess myself. I will live a holy and righteous life unto the Lord, walk according to His will, and fulfill my purpose. The Bible said we should let our light shine before others so they might see our good works and glorify the Father in heaven. When people see us, what do they see? Do they see question marks over our heads or the fruits of the Holy Spirit evident in us? We cannot fool God; we can only fool each other for a time. It doesn't make sense to live a life of pretense. Eventually, others will figure out who we really are. Rejoice in the Lord, and again, I said rejoice.

Scriptures for Your Reading and Admonition

For I know that this will turn out for my deliverance through your prayer and the supply of the Spirit of Jesus Christ. According to my earnest expectation and hope that in nothing I shall be ashamed, but with all boldness, as always, so now also Christ will be magnified in my body, whether by life or by death. For to me, to live is Christ, and to die is gain. But if I live on in the flesh, this will mean fruit from my labor; yet what I shall choose I cannot tell. For I am hard-pressed between the two, having a desire to depart and be with Christ, which is far better. Nevertheless, to remain in the flesh is more needful for you. And being confident of this, I know that I shall remain and continue with you all for your progress and joy of faith. That, your rejoicing for me may be more abundant in Jesus Christ by my coming to you again. Only let your conduct be worthy of the gospel of Christ, so that whether I come and see you or am absent, I may hear of your affairs, that you stand fast in one spirit, with one mind striving together for the faith of the gospel. And not in any way terrified by your adversaries, which is to them a proof of perdition, but to you of salvation, and that from God. For to you it has been granted on behalf of Christ, not only to believe in Him, but also to suffer for His sake. Having the same conflict which you saw in me and now hear is in me. (Philippians 1:19–30 NKJV)

I was so zealous that I harshly persecuted the church. And as for righteousness, I obeyed the law without fault. I once thought these things were valuable, but now I consider them worthless because of what Christ has done. Yes, everything else is worthless when compared with the infinite value of knowing Christ Jesus my Lord. For his sake I have discarded everything else, counting it all as garbage, so that I could gain Christ. And become one with him. I no longer count on my own righteousness through obeying the law; rather, I become righteous through faith in Christ. For God's way of making us right with himself depends on faith. I want to know Christ and experience the mighty power that raised him from the dead. I want to suffer with him, sharing in his death. So that one way or another I will experience the resurrection from the dead! I don't mean to say that I have already achieved these things or that I have already reached perfection. But I press on to possess that perfection for which Christ Jesus first possessed me. No, dear brothers, and sisters, I have not achieved it, but I focus on this one thing: Forgetting the past and looking forward to what lies ahead. I press on to reach the end of the race and receive the heavenly prize for which God, through Christ Jesus, is calling us. Let all who are spiritually mature agree on these things. If you disagree on some point, I believe God will make it plain to you. But we must hold on to the progress we have already made. Dear brothers and sisters, pattern your lives after mine, and learn from those who follow our example. For I have told you often before, and I say it again with tears in my eyes, that there are many whose conduct shows they are really enemies of the cross of Christ. They are headed for destruction. Their god is their appetite, they brag about shameful things, and they think only about this life here on earth. But we are citizens of heaven, where the Lord Jesus Christ lives. And we are eagerly waiting for him to return as our Savior. He will take our weak mortal bodies and change them into glorious bodies like his own, using the same power with which he will bring everything under his control. (Philippians 3:6–21 NLT)

And we know [with great confidence] that God [who is deeply concerned about us] causes all things to work together [as a plan] for good for those who love God, to those who are called according to His plan and purpose. For those whom He foreknew [and loved and chose beforehand], He also predestined to be conformed to the image of His Son [and ultimately share in His complete sanctification], so that He would be the firstborn [the most beloved and honored] among many believers. And those whom He predestined, He also called; and those whom He called, He also justified [declared free of the guilt of sin]; and those whom He justified, He also glorified [raising them to a heavenly dignity]. What then shall we say to all these things? If God is for us, who can be [successful] against us? He who did not spare

[even] His own Son, but gave Him up for us all, how will He not also, along with Him, graciously give us all things? Who will bring any charge against God's elect (His chosen ones)? It is God who justifies us [declaring us blameless and putting us in a right relationship with Himself]. Who is the one who condemns us? Christ Jesus is the One who died [to pay our penalty], and more than that, who was raised [from the dead], and who is at the right hand of God interceding [with the Father] for us. Who shall ever separate us from the love of Christ? Will tribulation, distress, or persecution, or famine, or nakedness, or danger, or sword? Just as it is written and forever remains written, "FOR YOUR SAKE WE ARE PUT TO DEATH ALL DAY LONG; WE ARE REGARDED AS SHEEP FOR THE SLAUGHTER." Yet in all these things we are more than conquerors and gain an overwhelming victory through Him who loved us [so much that He died for us]. For I am convinced [and continue to be convinced—beyond any doubt] that neither death, nor life, nor angels, nor principalities, nor things present and threatening, nor things to come, nor powers. Nor height, nor depth, nor any other created thing, will be able to separate us from the [unlimited] love of God, which is in Christ Jesus our Lord. (Romans 8:28–39 AMP)

I say then: Walk in the Spirit, and you shall not fulfill the lust of the flesh. For the flesh lusts against the Spirit, and the Spirit against the flesh; and these are contrary to one another, so that you do not do the things that you wish. But if you are led by the Spirit, you are not under the law. Now the works of the flesh are evident, which are: adultery, fornication, uncleanness, lewdness. Idolatry, sorcery, hatred, contentions, jealousies, outbursts of wrath, selfish ambitions, dissensions, heresies. Envy, murders, drunkenness, revelries, and the like; of which I tell you beforehand, just as I also told you in time past, that those who practice such things will not inherit the kingdom of God. But the fruit of the Spirit is love, joy, peace, longsuffering, kindness, goodness, faithfulness. Gentleness, self-control. Against such there is no law. And those who are Christ's have crucified the flesh with its passions and desires. If we live in the Spirit, let us also walk in the Spirit. Let us not become conceited, provoking one another, envying one another. (Galatians 5:16–26 NKJV)

So then, my dear ones, just as you have always obeyed [my instructions with enthusiasm], not only in my presence, but now much more in my absence, continue to work out your salvation [that is, cultivate it, bring it to full effect, actively pursue spiritual maturity] with awe-inspired fear and trembling [using serious caution and critical self-evaluation to avoid anything that might offend God or discredit the name of Christ]. For it is [not your strength, but it is] God who is effectively at work in you, both to will and to work [that is, strengthening, energizing, and creating in you the longing and the ability to fulfill your purpose] for His good pleasure. Do everything without murmuring or questioning [the providence of God]. So that you may prove yourselves to be blameless and guileless, innocent, and uncontaminated, children of God without blemish in the midst of a [morally] crooked and [spiritually] perverted generation, among whom you are seen as bright lights [beacons shining out clearly] in the world [of darkness.] Holding out and offering to everyone the word of life, so that in the day of Christ I will have reason to rejoice greatly because I did not run [my race] in vain nor labor without result. But even if I am being poured out as a drink offering on the sacrifice and service of your faith [for preaching the message of salvation], still I rejoice and share my joy with you all. You too, rejoice in the same way and share your joy with me. But I hope in the Lord Jesus to send Timothy to you soon, so that I may also be encouraged by learning news about you. For I have no one else [like him who is] so kindred a spirit who will be genuinely concerned for your [spiritual] welfare. For the others [who deserted me after my arrest] all seek [to advance] their own interests, not those of Jesus Christ. But you know of Timothy's tested worth and his proven character, that he has served with me to advance the gospel like a son serving with his father. Therefore, I hope [that it is His will] to send him immediately, just as soon as I see how my case turns out. (Philippians 2:12–23 AMP)

As for me, may I never boast about anything except the cross of our Lord Jesus Christ. Because of that cross, my interest in this world has been crucified, and the world's interest in me has also died. It doesn't matter whether we have been circumcised or not. What counts is whether we have been transformed into a new creation. May God's peace and mercy be upon all who live by this principle; they are the new people of God. (Galatians 6:14–16 NLT)

But God, who is rich in mercy, because of His great love with which He loved us. Even when we were dead in trespasses, made us alive together with Christ (by grace you have been saved). And raised us up together and made us sit together in the heavenly places in Christ Jesus. That in the ages to come He might show the exceeding riches of His grace in His kindness toward us in Christ Jesus. For by grace you have been saved through faith, and that not of yourselves; it is the gift of God. Not of works, lest anyone boast. For we are His workmanship, created in Christ Jesus for good works, which God prepared beforehand that we should walk in them. (Ephesians 2:4–10 NKJV)

Since you have been raised to new life with Christ, set your sights on the realities of heaven, where Christ sits in the place of honor at God's right hand. Think about the things of heaven, not the things of earth. For you died to this life, and your real life is hidden with Christ in God. And when Christ, who is your life, is revealed to the whole world, you will share in all his glory. So put to death the sinful, earthly things lurking within you. Have nothing to do with sexual immorality, impurity, lust, and evil desires. Don't be greedy, for a greedy person is an idolater, worshiping the things of this world. Because of these sins, the anger of God is coming. You used to do these things when your life was still part of this world. But now is the time to get rid of anger, rage, malicious behavior, slander, and dirty language. Don't lie to each other, for you have stripped off your old sinful nature and all its wicked deeds. Put on your new nature and be renewed as you learn to know your Creator and become like him. In this new life, it doesn't matter if you are a Jew or a Gentile, circumcised or uncircumcised, barbaric, uncivilized, slave, or free. Christ is all that matters, and he lives in all of us. Since God chose you to be the holy people he loves, you must clothe yourselves with tenderhearted mercy, kindness, humility, gentleness, and patience. Make allowance for each other's faults and forgive anyone who offends you. Remember, the Lord forgave you, so you must forgive others. Above all, clothe yourselves with love, which binds us all together in perfect harmony. And let the peace that comes from Christ rule in your hearts. For as members of one body, you are called to live in peace. And always be thankful. Let the message about Christ, in all its richness, fill your lives. Teach and counsel each other with all the wisdom he gives. Sing psalms and hymns and spiritual songs to God with thankful hearts. And whatever you do or say, do it as a representative of the Lord Jesus, giving thanks through him to God the Father. (Colossians 3:1–17 NLT)

Therefore, since Christ suffered in the flesh [and died for us], arm yourselves [like warriors] with the same purpose [being willing to suffer for doing what is right and pleasing God], because whoever has suffered in the flesh [being like-minded with Christ] is done with [intentional] sin [having stopped pleasing the world]. So that he can no longer spend the rest of his natural life living for human appetites and desires, but [lives] for the will and purpose of God. For the time already past is [more than] enough for doing what the [unsaved] Gentiles like to do—living [unrestrained as you have done] in a course of [shameless] sensuality, lusts, drunkenness, carousing, drinking parties, and wanton idolatries. In [connection with] all this, they [the unbelievers] are resentful and surprised that you do not [think like them, value their values and] run [hand in hand] with them into the same excesses of dissipation and immoral freedom, and they criticize and abuse and ridicule you and make fun of your values. But they will [must] give an account to Him who is ready to judge and pass sentence on the living and the dead. For this is why the good news [of salvation] was preached [in their lifetimes] even to those who are dead, that though they were judged in the flesh as men are, they may live in the spirit according to [the will and purpose of] God. The end and culmination of all things is near. Therefore, be sound-minded and self-controlled for the purpose of prayer [staying balanced and focused on the things of God so that your communication will be clear, reasonable, specific, and pleasing to Him.]. Above all, have fervent and unfailing love for one another, because love covers a multitude of sins [it overlooks unkindness and unselfishly seeks the best for others]. Be hospitable to one another without complaint. (1 Peter 4:1–9 AMP)

Likewise, you younger men [of lesser rank and experience], be subject to your elders [seek their counsel]; and all of you, clothe yourselves with humility toward one another [tie on the servant's apron], for GOD IS OPPOSED TO THE PROUD [the disdainful, the presumptuous, and He defeats them], BUT HE GIVES GRACE TO THE HUMBLE.

Therefore humble yourselves under the mighty hand of God [set aside self-righteous pride], so that He may exalt you [to a place of honor in His service] at the appropriate time. Casting all your cares [all your anxieties, all your worries, and all your concerns, once and for all] on Him, for He cares about you [with deepest affection, and watches over you very carefully]. Be sober [well balanced and self-disciplined be always alert and cautious. That enemy of yours, the devil, prowls around like a roaring lion [fiercely hungry], seeking someone to devour. But resist him, be firm in your faith [against his attack—rooted, established, immovable], knowing that the same experiences of suffering are being experienced by your brothers and sisters throughout the world. [You do not suffer alone.]. After you have suffered for a little while, the God of all grace [who imparts His blessing and favor], who called you to His own eternal glory in Christ, will Himself complete, confirm, strengthen, and establish you [making you what you ought to be]. To Him be dominion (power, authority, sovereignty) forever and ever. Amen. (1 Peter 5:5–11 AMP)

Since you have been raised to new life with Christ, set your sights on the realities of heaven, where Christ sits in the place of honor at God's right hand. Think about the things of heaven, not the things of earth. For you died to this life, and your real life is hidden with Christ in God. And when Christ, who is your life, is revealed to the whole world, you will share in all his glory. So put to death the sinful, earthly things lurking within you. Have nothing to do with sexual immorality, impurity, lust, and evil desires. Don't be greedy, for a greedy person is an idolater, worshiping the things of this world. Because of these sins, the anger of God is coming. You used to do these things when your life was still part of this world. But now is the time to get rid of anger, rage, malicious behavior, slander, and dirty language. Don't lie to each other, for you have stripped off your old sinful nature and all its wicked deeds. Put on your nature and be renewed as you learn to know your Creator and become like him. (Colossians 3:1–10 NLT)

So put aside every trace of malice and all deceit and hypocrisy and envy and all slander and hateful speech. Like newborn babies [you should] long for the pure milk of the word, so that by it you may be nurtured and grow in respect to salvation [its ultimate fulfillment]. If in fact you have [already] tasted the goodness and gracious kindness of the Lord. (1 Peter 2:1–3 AMP)

So I, the prisoner for the Lord, appeal to you to live a life worthy of the calling to which you have been called [that is, to live a life that exhibits godly character, moral courage, personal integrity, and mature behavior—a life that expresses gratitude to God for your salvation]. With all humility [forsaking self-righteousness], and gentleness [maintaining self-control], with patience, bearing with one another in [unselfish] love. Make every effort to keep the oneness of the Spirit in the bond of peace [each individual working together to make the whole successful]. There is one body [of believers] and one Spirit—just as you were called to one hope when called [to salvation]. One Lord, one faith, one baptism. One God and Father of us all who is [sovereign] overall and [working] through all and [living] in all. Yet grace [God's undeserved favor] was given to each one of us [not indiscriminately, but in different ways] in proportion to the measure of Christ's [rich and abundant] gift. Therefore it says, "WHEN HE ASCENDED ON HIGH, HE LED CAPTIVITY CAPTIVE, AND HE BESTOWED GIFTS ON MEN." Now this expression, "He ascended," what does it mean except that He also had previously descended [from the heights of heaven] into the lower parts of the earth? He who descended is the very same as He who also has ascended high above all the heavens, that He [His presence] might fill all things that is, the whole universe. And [His gifts to the church were varied and] He Himself appointed some as apostles [special messengers, representatives], some as prophets [who speak a new message from God to the people], some as evangelists [who spread the good news of salvation], and some as pastors and teachers [to shepherd and guide and instruct]. And He did this] to fully equip and perfect the saints (God's people) for works of service, to build up the body of Christ [the church]. Until we all reach oneness in the faith and in the knowledge of the Son of God, [growing spiritually] to become a mature believer, reaching to the measure of the fullness of Christ [manifesting His spiritual completeness and exercising our spiritual gifts in unity]. So that we are no longer children [spiritually immature], tossed back and forth [like ships on a stormy sea] and carried about by every wind of [shifting] doctrine, by the cunning and trickery of [unscrupulous] men, by the deceitful scheming of people ready to do anything [for personal profit]. But speaking the truth in love [in all things—both our speech and our lives expressing His truth], let us grow up in all things into Him [following His example] who is the Head—Christ. From Him the whole body [the church, in all its various parts], joined and knitted firmly together by what every joint supplies, when each part is working properly, causes the body to grow and mature, building itself up in [unselfish] love. So this I say, and solemnly affirm together with the Lord [as in His presence], that you must no longer live as the [unbelieving] Gentiles live, in the futility of their minds [and in the foolishness and emptiness of their souls]. For their [moral] understanding is darkened, and their reasoning is clouded; [they are] alienated and self-banished from the life of God [with no share in it; this is] because of the [willful] ignorance and spiritual blindness that is [deep-seated] within them, because of the hardness and insensitivity of their heart. And they, [the ungodly in their spiritual apathy], having become callous and unfeeling, have given themselves over [as prey] to unbridled sensuality, eagerly craving the practice of every kind of impurity [that their desires may demand]. But you did not learn Christ in this way! If in fact you have [really] heard Him and have been taught by Him, just as truth is in Jesus [revealed in His life and personified in Him]. That, regarding your previous way of life, you put off your old self [completely discard your former nature], which is being corrupted through deceitful desires. And be continually renewed in the spirit of your mind [having a fresh, untarnished mental and spiritual attitude]. And put on the new self [the regenerated and renewed nature], created in God's image, [godlike] in the righteousness and holiness of the truth [living in a way that expresses to God your gratitude for your salvation]. Therefore, rejecting all falsehood [whether lying, defrauding, telling half-truths, spreading rumors, any such as these], SPEAK TRUTH EACH ONE WITH HIS NEIGHBOR, for we are all parts of one another [and we are all parts of the body of Christ]. BE ANGRY [at sin—at immorality, at injustice, at ungodly behavior], YET DO NOT SIN; do not let your anger [cause you shame, nor allow it to] last until the sun goes down. And do not give the devil an opportunity [to lead you into sin by holding a grudge, or nurturing anger, or harboring resentment, or cultivating bitterness]. The thief [who has become a believer] must no longer steal, but instead he must work hard [making an honest living], producing that which is good with his own hands, so that he will have something to share with those in need. Do not let unwholesome [foul, profane, worthless, vulgar] words ever come out of your mouth, but only such speech as is good for building up others, according to the need and the occasion, so that it will be a blessing to those who hear [you speak]. And do not grieve the Holy Spirit of God [but seek to please Him], by whom you were sealed and marked [branded as God's own] for the day of redemption [the final deliverance from the consequences of sin]. Let all bitterness and wrath and anger and clamor [perpetual animosity, resentment, strife, fault-finding] and slander be put away from you, along with every kind of malice [all spitefulness, verbal abuse, malevolence]. Be kind and helpful to one another, tender-hearted [compassionate, understanding], forgiving one another [readily and freely], just as God in Christ also forgave you. (Ephesians 4:1–32 AMP)

My old self has been crucified with Christ. It is no longer I who live, but Christ lives in me. So, I live in this earthly body by trusting in the Son of God, who loved me and gave himself for me. I do not treat the grace of God as meaningless. For if keeping the law could make us right with God, then there was no need for Christ to die. (Galatians 2:20–21 NLT)

HEAVEN IS TOO IMPORTANT TO MISS

As we unfold the words of the Father through his Son Jesus Christ, we appreciate and understand the message of the Kingdom of heaven, which has been ignored, neglected, and pushed aside for something that is glamorous and appeasing to the flesh. The true message that's been missing has been rekindled once again in the hearts of the minority. We purpose in our hearts to do what is right, so we will be qualified to enter the eternal Kingdom of God, where life continues for all eternity. Many have embraced something different than the original message: the message of the Kingdom of heaven that was commanded and given to the church to teach and preach. Let us understand the structure of the *constitution* by which we live our lives as children in the Kingdom of God.

The members of the Trinity serve each other. All defer to one another and yet they are *one*. The Son says what He hears from the Father (John 12:49–50). The Father witnesses to and glorifies the Son (John 8:16, 29, 54). The Father and Son honor the Holy Spirit by commissioning Him to speak in their name (John 14:16, 26). The Holy Spirit honors the Father and Son by helping and enabling the community of citizens to live the life required by scriptures.

What is the Kingdom of God? The Kingdom of God is not a religious entity or a political party. The Kingdom of God is the sovereign rule and governing influence of the King over His territory.

He impacts it with His will, culture, and purpose, producing a citizenry of people who reflect the King's culture and manifest His nature.

That is why Jesus Christ taught and demonstrated with signs, miracles, and wonders while He walked the earth during His ministry.

> Now when it was day, He departed and went into a deserted place. And the crowd sought Him and came to Him and tried to keep Him from leaving them;. But He said to them, "I must preach the kingdom of God to the other cities also, because for this purpose I have been sent. (Luke 4:42–43 NKJV)

The beginning and declaration of the message of the kingdom of heaven was heard from the mouth of John the Baptist, the forerunner of our Lord Jesus Christ (Matthew 3:1–3). He began his preaching with the words, "Prepare the way of the Lord, make his paths straight." He had a burning awareness of the one who was to come after him and who would be baptize in the Holy Spirit and fire. John was a reformer and preached of messianic hope through the message of the kingdom of heaven/God. He was the herald who came. He sought to make the hearts of the people ready for our King and Lord.

John called the people away from the comforts of their homes and towns, out into the wilderness where they might meet God. The wilderness was where God had previously dwelled with His people after the Exodus. The conviction that God was about to begin a new work among this unprepared people broke upon John with the force of urgency. John's efforts at moral reform, symbolized by baptism, were his way of preparing Israel to meet their God.

The message of John's moral challenge is hard for many to appreciate today. His command to share clothing and food (Luke 3:11) was a painful slap in the face to a society hungry to acquire material assets and wealth.

When he warned the tax collectors not to take more money than they had coming to them (Luke 3:12–13), he exposed the greed in the hearts of the hearers, which had drawn them to such positions in the first place. The soldiers (today's police and prison officers) he told to be content with their wages must have winced at the thought of not using their power to take advantage of the common people (Luke 3:14–16). Not much has changed since then. That is why the message of the Kingdom has been ignored by the masses over the years. Many people believe that because the message of the Kingdom is in the minority, it is not the true message for today.

Let me disturb the way you think for a while. Where in the scriptures does it say the majority is correct? Noah and his household of eight altogether were correct. Only Noah and his household entered the ark, while thousands neglected the message and were destroyed when the flood occurred. Of the twelve spies who went to investigate the land, ten brought back negative reports. Two said they could take the land because God said so. Which group was correct? Elijah the prophet spoke against the 450 false prophets of Baal on Mount Carmel. Who was correct? Jesus spoke of two gates, and said to enter the narrow gateway; only a few would make it. Which group will enter the eternal Kingdom? Paul was on a ship heading to Rome. Including Paul, there were 276 men on board. There was a storm. Paul said the angel of the Lord stood by him and said if anyone jumps over, he shall perish. Who was correct? Of the seven churches in Revelation chapters 2 and 3, five were called to repent. How much of this is correct? From Abel to the Day of Judgment, most of God's creation will be going to the lake of fire. They refuse to acknowledge the saving grace of God in Christ Jesus and live lives acceptable to God according to His word.

That's why in the church, there is not supposed to be voting at the end of meetings to see which group is right or wrong. The angel of the house has the final say about what is right or wrong. Voting is a worldly mechanism being used to determine the outcome of many situations in politics, business, sports, legal proceedings, and religion.

After John the Baptist baptized Jesus, the heavens opened and the Holy Spirit descended upon Him and remained. The voice of the Father proclaimed, "This is my beloved Son in whom I'm pleased." Jesus pleased his Father for thirty years. What about you? Is your life right with the Father? Can He boast about you today? Immediately, Jesus was led into the wilderness to prepare Himself for the passing of the baton. He had to receive it from the forerunner John the Baptist to fulfill His purpose and the Father's will for His life.

Mark 1:14–15 tells us that Jesus began His ministry right after John was cast into prison. He received the right hand of fellowship and the baton from his forerunner John. He began to preach the same message as John once did with a little swing in it. He said the time was fulfilled and the kingdom of God was at hand. He told people to repent and believe the gospel. Jesus was and is the embodiment of the Kingdom of heaven. Jesus knew His responsibilities were great and He needed help. He chose twelve men from his everyday walk. They were from different industries, had different levels of education, and had different values and principles in their own ways of living. He called people like you and me, and said, "Come follow me and I'll make you fishers of men." Jesus taught these men the things of the Kingdom of God for a period of three and a half years, and they still didn't have it right. It was only after His death and resurrection they got it right. When He called them, they became His followers, leaders of people, and agents of change. They made the necessary sacrifices and became carriers of the anointing.

During those times, the disciples were preparing and being schooled by Jesus. He chose three to be His inner circle, not His bodyguards. He needed no protection from anyone. In Matthew 5:3–16, the Sermon on the Mount, Jesus outlined some key values, the principles and characteristics of the Kingdom of God. Jesus taught that to evangelize the earth, we must have experienced hearts, which will lead us to transformation. Our outer bodies will reflect our inner beings.

Jesus was fulfilling His purpose and the Father's will by remaining obedient to the mission. The disciples witnessed many miracles, even on the Sabbath day. They understood the things of the Kingdom at a certain level. The most familiar statement of these principles is in Matthew 5:7, which Jesus addressed to His disciples. These principles showed how those who were already children of the Kingdom ought to live. One was that the merciful are blessed because they shall obtain mercy. As children of the Kingdom, we ought to have forgiving spirits to obtain mercy, as in Matthew 6:12.

Jesus insisted that more is expected of his followers than from the scribes and Pharisees who represent the world. Our ethical behavior and righteousness should exceed the righteousness of the scribes and Pharisees (Matthew 5:20). Otherwise, we will definitely not enter the Kingdom of heaven. Jesus actually threatened His people in this verse. If we really want to enter the Kingdom of heaven, we definitely have to step up our righteousness.

The Pharisees were a religious and political party in Palestine in New Testament times. They were known for insisting that the law of God be observed as the scribes interpreted it. This was because it was in their favor and because of their special commitment to keeping the laws of tithing and ritual purity. The scribes were members of a learned class in ancient Israel through New Testament times who studied the scriptures and served as copyists, editors, and teachers. They were all lobbyists and lovers of money.

If you love only those who love you, Jesus asked, what credit is that to you? Even sinners love those who love them (Luke 6:26–38). The higher standard of the Kingdom of God called for acts of love to enemies, and words of blessing and goodwill to persecutors. The children of the Kingdom should not insist on their legal rights but cheerfully give them up in response to the supreme law of love.

In Matthew 5, Jesus indicates that after someone has done all in his or her power to bring about the necessary transformation through application of the mentioned values and principles, he or she ought to be in a place of perfection. A person should be perfect even as the heavenly Father is perfect. Perfection is a place of maturity, where nothing moves the person. When trials, hardship, persecution, lack comes someone's way, because of maturity in God, the person will be able to embrace all of it and stand still to see the salvation of God.

As Portia says in Shakespeare's *The Merchant of Venice*, "The quality of mercy is not strain'd; It droppeth as the gentle rain from heaven upon the place beneath. It is twice blest: It blesseth him that gives and him that takes."[2] Mercy falls on the just and the unjust, for God's mercy endures for a thousand generations. In order to obtain mercy, a person has to show mercy. Jesus's first word in Matthew 4:17 deals with mercy. He told people to *repent* and that He came with the power and authority to forgive people of any and all of their sins. "You can call Me mercy."

When Jesus said to repent, He meant He came on behalf of the Father of Spirits and according to the promise He made in Genesis 3:15. He came to bring people back to that place of innocence where Adam was before he disobeyed the Father. That's why the message John the Baptist preached in Luke 3:11–19 was difficult for people to embrace. The enemy of human nature is obedience, because people were born in sin and shaped in iniquity. For someone to come back into alignment takes a lot of discipline, self-control, prayer, and fasting. Because God is merciful, He expects His children to be merciful they have obtained mercy. we must do all in our power to enter the everlasting Kingdom prepared for His children, those who love Him. Love brings obedience. Each person has the passport

---

[2] William Shakespeare, *The Merchant of Venice* (London, 1597; Project Gutenberg, May 22, 2019), https://www.gutenberg.org/cache/epub/1779/pg1779-images.html.

(confession) but not the *heavenly visa*, which is doing the will of the Father. That will give a person full access to the Kingdom of God.

After time elapsed and the disciples had been taught, they were excited and ready for evangelism. Jesus called them and gave them power.

And when He had called His twelve disciples to Him, He gave them power over unclean spirits, to cast them out, and to heal all kinds of sickness and all kinds of disease. These twelve Jesus sent out and commanded them, saying: "Do not go into the way of the Gentiles, and do not enter a city of the Samaritans. But go rather to the lost sheep of the house of Israel. And as you go, preach, saying, the kingdom of heaven is at hand. Heal the sick, cleanse the lepers, raise the dead, cast out demons. Freely you have received, freely give. (Matthew 10:1, 5–8 NKJV)

Jesus gave the twelve disciples their first assignment. He emphasized that they should not change the message they heard Him teach and which He gave to them. They were not to go to the Samaritans and the Gentiles, but to the lost sheep of Israel. Salvation was only for the covenant people, not for dogs. Salvation was never for us. It was meant only for the Jewish nation, but they have rejected their Messiah, Jesus. We have to thank God and be grateful that they rejected Jesus so we could be grafted to the olive branch.

The disciples carried the message of the Kingdom throughout the land to the lost sheep of Israel. They didn't preach about healing, transformation, or salvation, but about the Kingdom. When you preach the message of the Kingdom, you are literally preaching everything that the Kingdom has to offer you. This includes peace of mind, healing for all manner of sicknesses and diseases, deliverance from death and demon possession, hope for a better tomorrow, eternal rest for your soul and the souls of your loved ones, provision for your earthly needs, and everything that's good and perfect.

Jesus said in Luke 22:29 (NKJV), "And I bestow upon you a kingdom, just as My Father bestowed one upon Me." The nature of this Kingdom is determined by the character of the God whose Kingdom it is. The revelation of God lay at the very heart of Jesus's teaching. Jesus called Him Father and taught His disciples to do the same. However, the term He used when He called God Father was Abba (Mark 14:36). It was not unusual for God to be addressed in prayer as Heavenly Father. Jesus taught His followers to look to God with the trust that children show when they expect their earthly fathers to provide them with food, clothes, and shelter. Works of mercy and power, healing of the sick, and deliverance for those who were demon-possessed accompanied Jesus's proclamation of the Kingdom of God.

These works also proclaimed the arrival of the Kingdom of God. The demons that caused such distress to men and women were signs of the kingdom of Satan. When they were cast out, this proved the superior power and authority of the Kingdom of God. This message and demonstration of the Kingdom brought Jesus into conflict with the scribes and Pharisees. The scribes were the official teachers of the law. Because of their influence, He was barred from preaching and teaching in the synagogues. This was no great inconvenience to Jesus. He simply gathered larger congregations to listen to Him on the hillsides and by the lakeshores.

The religious leaders and teachers found much of Jesus's activity disturbing. He refused to be bound by their religious beliefs and ideas. He befriended those who were considered outcasts in society. Jesus insisted on applying the law of God in the light of its original intention, not according to the popular interpretation of the religious leaders and high priests. He insisted on healing sick people on the Sabbath day. He also believed that healing people did not profane the Sabbath but honored it because it was established by God for the rest and relief of human beings (Luke 6:5–10).

In a similar way, Jesus settled the question of divorce by an appeal to the original marriage ordinance, outlined in Genesis 1:26 and 2:24–25. Since husband and wife were made one by the Creator's decree, Jesus pointed out that divorce was an attempt to undo and remove God's original meaning and purpose. The law through Moses later allowed for divorce in certain situations, which was a concession to the hardness of people's hearts and their inability to keep the commandments. However, it was not so in the beginning, Jesus declared, and it should not be so for those who belong to the Kingdom of God. In appealing to that original purpose, Jesus declared that a commandment was most faithfully obeyed when God's purpose in giving it was and is fulfilled.

Children of God, whose confession is in the Lord Jesus Christ, should reproduce their Heavenly Father's character. He does not discriminate between the good and the evil in bestowing rain and sunshine. Likewise, His children should not discriminate in showing kindness to all. He delights in forgiving sinners. His children should also be marked by a forgiving spirit.

The example of the heavenly Father and the example shown by Jesus on earth are one and the same because Jesus came to reveal the Father. Jesus's life was the practical demonstration of the Father's teaching and works. To His disciples, He declared,

> You call Me Teacher and Lord, and you say well, for so I am. If I then, your Lord and Teacher, have washed your feet, you also ought to wash one another's feet. For I have given you an example, that you should do as I have done to you. Most assuredly, I say to you, a servant is not greater than his master; nor is he who is sent greater than he who sent him. If you know these things, blessed are you if you do them. (John 13:13–17 NKJV)

First John 2:3–6 (AMP) tells us,

> And this is how we know [daily, by experience] that
> we have come to know Him [to understand Him
> and be more deeply acquainted with Him]: if we
> habitually keep [focused on His precepts and obey]
> His commandments (teachings). Whoever says, "I
> have come to know Him," but does not habitually
> keep [focused on His precepts and obey] His
> commandments (teachings), is a liar, and the truth
> [of the divine word] is not in him. But whoever
> habitually keeps His word and obeys His precepts
> [and treasures His message in its entirety], in him the
> love of God has truly been perfected [it is completed
> and has reached maturity]. By this we know [for
> certain] that we are in Him. Whoever says he lives
> in Christ [that is, whoever says he has accepted Him
> as God and Savior] ought [as a moral obligation] to
> walk and conduct himself just as He walked and
> conducted Himself.

Jesus's ethical teaching was part of His proclamation of the Kingdom of God. Only by His death and resurrection could the divine rule be established. However, even while the Kingdom of God was in the process of inauguration during His ministry, its principles could be translated into action in the lives of His followers.

In the Kingdom of God, the way to honor is the way of service. In this respect, Jesus set a worthy example, choosing to give service instead of receive it. The death and resurrection of Jesus unleashed the Kingdom of God in full power. Through proclamation of the Kingdom, liberation and blessing were brought to many more than who could have been touched by Jesus's brief ministry.

The priority of the Kingdom, and the number one goal of all humanity, should be to enter the Kingdom of God. To enter means to pursue and attain citizenship in the Kingdom of heaven. Citizenship gives people access to what is available in the Kingdom. This includes the King as well as keys, an army, a constitution, an economy, taxes, a health care system, privileges, rights, principles, a culture, ambassadors, and society.

The greatest tragedy in life is not death but living a life without Jesus as your Lord and Savior. You eventually die in your sin. Hebrews 9:27 (NKJV) declares, "And as it is appointed for men to die once, but after this the judgment." There must be a public alliance in the acceptance of Jesus as Lord, in accordance with Matthew 10:32–33 (NLT), which states, "Everyone who acknowledges me publicly here on earth, I will also acknowledge before my Father in heaven. But everyone who denies me here on earth, I will also deny before my Father in heaven."

In addition, Romans 10:8–11 (AMP) states,

> But what does it say? "THE WORD IS NEAR YOU, IN YOUR MOUTH AND IN YOUR HEART"—that is, the word [the message, the basis] of faith which we preach. Because if you acknowledge and confess with your mouth that Jesus is Lord [recognizing His power, authority, and majesty as God], and believe in your heart that God raised Him from the dead, you will be saved. For with the heart a person believes [in Christ as Savior] resulting in his justification [that is, being made righteous—being freed of the guilt of sin and made acceptable to God]; and with the mouth he acknowledges and confesses [his faith openly], resulting in and confirming [his] salvation. For the Scripture says, "WHOEVER BELIEVES IN HIM [whoever adheres to, trusts in, and relies on Him] WILL NOT BE DISAPPOINTED [in his expectations]."

Let's make it our first priority in life to diligently seek and *truly* discover, enter, understand, experience, live, demonstrate, communicate, and publicize the Good News of the Kingdom of God that Christ established and gave to us. This is the same Kingdom He ordered and commissioned us to publicize.

If the church of Christ in the present time would renew its vitality and increase the effectiveness of its evangelism, then we could return to a greater emphasis upon that which we have heard from the beginning.

Those who profess to know God need to examine themselves by asking the following. Do I really possess a strong desire for God, His presence, and the commission which I received from Him in my life? Or do I go through life largely consumed with secular pursuits and worldly entertainment, while prayer and fasting, fervent love for Jesus, study of God's word, and a deep desire for God and His Kingdom have little place or vitality in my affections and time?

As water is essential for physical life, so God and His presence are essential for satisfaction and wholeness of life. As Psalm 42:1–2 (NLT) states, "As the deer longs for streams of water, so I long for you, O God. I thirst for God, the living God. When can I go and stand before him?" Every believer should pray as David did in this psalm. It describes a man's deep longing in his heart for God, a heart that can only be satisfied by an intimate relationship with Him. In Psalm 63:1–6 (NLT), we read,

> O God, you are my God; I earnestly search for you. My soul thirsts for you; my whole-body longs for you in this parched and weary land where there is no water. I have seen you in your sanctuary and gazed upon your power and glory. Your unfailing love is better than life itself; how I praise you! I will praise you as long as I live, lifting my hands to you in prayer. You satisfy me more than the richest feast. I will praise you with songs of joy. I lie awake thinking of you, meditating on you through the night.

We need the Lord more than ever at this time in history. Just look around you and understand what's going on; there's trouble on every side. The Bible says because *iniquity/lawlessness* shall abound, the love of many shall wax cold.

Alas (used to express sorrow or pity), how many there are who manifest no hunger or thirst after the things of God? What shall be said of this innumerable multitude? Why do they feel no hunger and no thirst? Like the absence of ordinary hunger, this spiritual lack of hunger is due to the awful cancer of sin gnawing (persistent and troubling or uncomfortable) out the heart of the victim. Others, already in the final throes/struggles of spiritual starvation, are past hunger and thirst. Some have perverted their desires and have no true hunger and thirst for spiritual things remaining. The ravages of disease, perversion, and starvation are thus able to destroy that eagerness of the soul that people should have for the things of God.

The Christian's hunger for the things of God is destroyed by worldly anxiety, the deceitfulness of wealth (Matthew 13:22 AMP), the desire for things (Mark 4:19 AMP), life's pleasures (Luke 8:14 AMP), and failure to abide in Christ (John 15:4 AMP). When the hunger of believers for God and His righteousness is destroyed, they will die spiritually (1 Timothy 5:5–6 AMP). For this reason, it is essential that we be sensitive to the Holy Spirit's convicting work in our lives.

The desire for righteousness is the only desire of people that can be truly and finally satisfied. Appetites of the flesh, all of them, can be satisfied only for the moment. Hebrews 11:25–27 (NLT) says of Moses,

> He chose to share the oppression of God's people instead of enjoying the fleeting pleasures of sin. He thought it was better to suffer for the sake of Christ than to own the treasures of Egypt, for he was looking ahead to his great reward. It was by

faith that Moses left the land of Egypt, not fearing the king's anger. He kept right on going because he kept his eyes on the one who is invisible.

The drunkard, for example, never satisfies his or her thirst, but must die, at last, still unsatisfied. Physical hunger also cannot be satisfied, except for the moment. Death is always the result, whatever the cause, when the hunger of body cells can no longer be met. The heart that is fitted for communion is a hungering and thirsting heart. If you would have Christ with you, seek Him boldly. Let nothing hold you back. Defy the world. Press on where others flee. We ought to seek Christ faithfully, and now is the right time for you.

As recorded in Matthew 16:24–26 (AMP), Jesus taught that following Him involves heavy obligations concerning righteousness, acceptance of persecution, love for enemies, and self-denial. We must deny ourselves in order to follow Jesus. We have to sincerely endeavor to obey His commands, earnestly seek His kingdom and His righteousness, and persevere until the end in true faith, love, and purity, and even if it requires our lives.

Then Jesus said to His disciples, "If anyone wishes to follow Me [as My disciple], he must deny himself [set aside selfish interests], and take up his cross [expressing a willingness to endure whatever may come] and follow Me [believing in Me, conforming to My example in living and, if need be, suffering or perhaps dying because of faith in Me]. For whoever wishes to save his life [in this world] will [eventually] lose it [through death], but whoever loses his life [in this world] for My sake will find it [that is, life with Me for all eternity]. For what will it profit a man if he gains the whole world [wealth, fame, success], but forfeits his soul? Or what will a man give in exchange for his soul?

According to Matthew 6:19–21 and 30–34 (AMP), those who follow Christ are urged to "seek above all else" God's Kingdom and His righteousness. The verb *seek* implies being continually absorbed in a search for something or making a strenuous and diligent effort to obtain something.

> Do not store up for yourselves [material] treasures on earth, where moth and rust destroy, and where thieves break in and steal. But store up for yourselves treasures in heaven, where neither moth nor rust destroys, and where thieves do not break in and steal. For where your treasure is, there your heart [your wishes, your desires; that on which your life centers] will be also. But if God so clothes the grass of the field, which is alive and green today and tomorrow is [cut and] thrown [as fuel] into the furnace, will He not much more clothe you? You of little faith! Therefore do not worry or be anxious (perpetually uneasy, distracted), saying, "What are we going to eat?" or "What are we going to drink?" or "What are we going to wear?" For the [pagan] Gentiles eagerly seek all these things; [but do not worry,] for your heavenly Father knows that you need them. But first and most importantly seek (aim at, strive after) His kingdom and His righteousness [His way of doing and being right—the attitude and character of God], and all these things will be given to you also. So do not worry about tomorrow; for tomorrow will worry about itself. Each day has enough trouble of its own.

Deuteronomy 30:19 (NKJV) says, "Today I have given you the choice between life and death, between blessings and curses. Now I call on heaven and earth to witness the choice you make. Oh, that you would choose life, so that you and your descendants might live!"

Joshua 24:14–15 (AMP) says,

> "Now, therefore, fear the LORD and serve Him in sincerity and in truth; remove the gods which your fathers served on the other side of the [Euphrates] River and in Egypt, and serve the LORD. If it is unacceptable in your sight to serve the LORD, choose for yourselves this day whom you will serve: whether the gods which your fathers served that were on the other side of the river, or the gods of the Amorites in whose land you live; but as for me and my house, we will serve the LORD."

At this point in this book, you are already without excuse. Running from the Lord makes no sense. Stop running and give Him your heart today. Stop looking for people to like you when you are standing for righteousness. Stop thinking about what they might say about you, because you choose to live for the Lord from this day forward. What they might say is irrelevant and not important. What the Father of Spirits thinks and says about you is important.

Are you genuinely ready to surrender to the
Lord before it's too late for you?

Here is a prayer of repentance.

My Father, my father, I come before you in humility and with a sincere heart. I acknowledge that I am a sinner in need of your help and forgiveness of my sins. Lord, I repent of all my sins, and my unrighteous behaviors. I am sorry I acted in arrogance. Please have mercy upon me and forgive me of all sins and inequities. I confess Jesus as Lord and Redeemer over my life. I ask that you fill me with your Holy Spirit and give me grace and strength to live the life that will be pleasing to you in Jesus's name in prayer, amen.

It's not magic; it is only *faith*. You are born again, and I welcome you into the Kingdom of Heaven, for the Bible says, that heaven rejoices over one sinner who comes to Jesus.

Because you have supported me through the purchase of this book, I pronounce a blessing over you and your generations in the name of Jesus Christ of Nazareth, and in accordance with Numbers 6:24–26 (AMP).

> The LORD bless you, and keep you [protect you, sustain you, and guard you]. The LORD makes His face shine upon you [with favor] and be gracious to you [surrounding you with lovingkindness]. The LORD lift His countenance (face) upon you [with divine approval], and give you peace [a tranquil heart and life].

Just receive it by faith. Amen.

Scriptures for Your Reading and Admonition

> "The time is surely coming," says the Sovereign LORD, "when I will send a famine on the land—not a famine of bread or water but of hearing the words of the LORD. People will stagger from sea to sea and wander from border to border searching for the word of the LORD, but they will not find it. Beautiful girls and strong young men will grow faint in that day, thirsting for the LORD's word." (Amos 8:11–13 NLT)

Blessed is he who reads and those who hear the words of this prophecy and keep those things which are written in it; for the time is near. (Revelation 1:3 NKJV)

Sow with a view to righteousness [that righteousness, like seed, may germinate]; Reap in accordance with mercy and lovingkindness. Break up your uncultivated ground, For it is time to seek and search diligently for the Lord [and to long for His blessing] Until He comes to rain righteousness and His gift of salvation on you. (Hosea 10:12 AMP)

Search for the Lord and for his strength; continually seek him. (Psalm 105:4 NLT)

Everyone who thirsts, come to the waters; and you who have no money come, buy grain, and eat. Come, buy wine and milk without money and without cost [simply accept it as a gift from God]. Why do you spend money for which is not bread, and your earnings on what does not satisfy? Listen carefully to Me, and eat what is good, and let your soul delight in abundance. Seek the Lord while He may be found; Call on Him [for salvation] while He is near. (Isaiah 55:1–2 and 6 AMP)

And it is impossible to please God without faith. Anyone who wants to come to him must believe that God exists and that he rewards those who sincerely seek him. (Hebrews 11:6 NLT)

But from there you will seek the Lord your God, and you will find Him if you seek Him with all your

heart and with all your soul. (Deuteronomy 4:29
NKJV)

I cry out to God; yes, I shout. Oh, that God would
listen to me! When I was in deep trouble, I searched
for the Lord. All night long I prayed, with hands
lifted toward heaven, but my soul was not comforted.
I think of God, and I moan, overwhelmed with
longing for his help. (Psalm 77:1–3 NLT)

For whoever finds me finds life and obtains favor
from the Lord. But he who sins against me wrongs
his own soul; all those who hate me love death.
(Proverbs 8:35–36 NKJV)

And this is how we know [daily, by experience]
that we have come to know Him [to understand
Him and be more deeply acquainted with Him]:
if we habitually keep [focused on His precepts and
obey] His commandments (teachings). Whoever
says, "I have come to know Him," but does
not habitually keep [focused on His precepts and
obey] His commandments (teachings), is a liar, and
the truth [of the divine word] is not in him. But
whoever habitually keeps His word and obeys His
precepts [and treasures His message in its entirety],
in him the love of God has truly been perfected [it
is completed and has reached maturity]. By this we
know [for certain] that we are in Him. Whoever
says he lives in Christ [that is, whoever says he has
accepted Him as God and Savior] ought [as a moral
obligation] to walk and conduct himself just as He
walked and conducted Himself. (1 John 2:3–6 AMP)

Keep me from lying to myself; give me the privilege of knowing your instructions. I have chosen to be faithful; I have determined to live by your regulations...Your laws are my treasure; they are my heart's delight. I am determined to keep your decrees to the very end...Let praise flow from my lips, for you have taught me your decrees. Let my tongue sing about your word, for all your commands are right. Give me a helping hand, for I have chosen to follow your commandments. O LORD, I have longed for your rescue, and your instructions are my delight. Let me live so I can praise you, and may your regulations help me. I have wandered away like a lost sheep; come and find me, for I have not forgotten your commands. (Psalm 119:29–30, 111–112, and 171–176)

Therefore, since we are surrounded by so great a cloud of witnesses [who by faith have testified to the truth of God's absolute faithfulness], stripping off every unnecessary weight and the sin which so easily and cleverly entangles us, let us run with endurance and active persistence the race that is set before us. [looking away from all that will distract us and] focusing our eyes on Jesus, who is the Author and Perfecter of faith [the first incentive for our belief and the One who brings our faith to maturity], who for the joy [of accomplishing the goal] set before Him endured the cross, disregarding the shame, and sat down at the right hand of the throne of God [revealing His deity, His authority, and the completion of His work]. Just consider and meditate on Him who endured from sinners such bitter hostility toward Himself [consider it all in comparison with your trials], so that you will not grow weary and lose heart. (Hebrews 12:1–3 AMP)

No one who abides in Him [who remains united in fellowship with Him—deliberately, knowingly, and habitually] practices sin. No one who habitually sins have seen Him or known Him. Little children (believers, dear ones) do not let anyone lead you astray. The one who practices righteousness [the one who strives to live a consistently honorable life— in private as well as in public—and to conform to God's precepts] is righteous, just as He is righteous. The one who practices sin [separating himself from God, and offending Him by acts of disobedience, indifference, or rebellion] is of the devil [and takes his inner character and moral values from him, not God]; for the devil has sinned and violated God's law from the beginning. The Son of God appeared for this purpose, to destroy the works of the devil. No one who is born of God [deliberately, knowingly, and habitually] practices sin, because God's seed [His principle of life, the essence of His righteous character] remains [permanently] in him [who is born again—who is reborn from above—spiritually transformed, renewed, and set apart for His purpose]; and he [who is born again] cannot habitually [live a life characterized by] sin, because he is born of God and longs to please Him. By this the children of God and the children of the devil are clearly identified: anyone who does not practice righteousness [who does not seek God's will in thought, action, and purpose] is not of God, nor is the one who does not [unselfishly] love his [believing] brother. (1 John 3:6–10 AMP)

They will hunger no longer, nor thirst anymore; nor will the sun beat down on them, nor any [scorching] heat. For the Lamb who is in the center of the throne will be their Shepherd, and He will guide them to springs of the waters of life; and God will wipe every tear from their eyes [giving them eternal comfort]. (Revelation 7:16–17 AMP)

"Behold, I (Jesus) am coming quickly, and My reward is with Me, to give to each one according to the merit of his deeds (earthly works, faithfulness). I am the Alpha and the Omega, the First and the Last, the Beginning and the End [the Eternal One]. Blessed (happy, prosperous, to be admired) are those who wash their robes [in the blood of Christ by believing and trusting in Him—the righteous who do His commandments], so that they may have the right to the tree of life and may enter by the gates into the city. Outside are the dogs [the godless, the impure, those of low moral character] and the sorcerers [with their intoxicating drugs, and magic arts], and the immoral persons [the perverted, the molesters, and the adulterers], and the murderers, and the idolaters, and everyone who loves and practices lying (deception, cheating)." (Revelation 22:12–15 AMP)

BIBLIOGRAPHY

Dyer, Samuel. "Loving Arms." Dyers Promotions. September 9, 2011. YouTube video, 5:12. https://www.youtube.com/watch?v=ngyTBMWLqvI.

Shakespeare, William. *The Merchant of Venice*. London, 1597; Project Gutenberg, May 22, 2019. https://www.gutenberg.org/cache/epub/1779/pg1779-images.html.

ABOUT THE AUTHOR

I was born on the twin islands of Trinidad and Tobago, West Indies, in a small community called Liverpool circular Temple Street Arima. I am the son of George and Jean Hamilton, who had four sons, of which I am the youngest. George Hamilton passed away on May 9, 2017 and went home to be with the Lord. I have served the Lord for twenty-six years faithfully, and left a good testimony. I thank God for my earthly dad and the time I spent with him. As a dad, he has truly been an inspiration to me. He didn't have much money, but he was a genuine individual. I loved him with my whole heart, and one day I will rejoice with him in the presence of our King. For now, I must run my course faithfully and finish the work entrusted to me by my heavenly Father.

As a young man, even while living in sin and ignorance, I would say to myself and to my friend Phillip La Croix, "There is more to life than that which we are doing." I realized that there is purpose for being alive even in my ignorance.

To understand purpose and Kingdom, I concluded that I had to come back to the one who is responsible for me. That wasn't my parents, but God. I needed to go back to the garden where it all began. Purpose was created in the garden and the Kingdom was given to humankind. God created humankind to have dominion over His creation, not over each other. The statement I made in the above paragraph has propelled me to make the most important decision I have ever made and will ever make in my entire life. I decided to stop running and surrender all to Jesus Christ of Nazareth.

At the age of twenty-three, I gave my life to Jesus Christ and have never looked back, despite all the difficulties, hardships, trials, living in lack, temptations, and persecutions I've been through. God's mercies and His love have kept me through it all.

To my Heavenly Father, I just want to say thank you for saving me. Thank you for your Son Jesus Christ and His shed blood. Thank you for your Holy Spirit teaching and guiding me into all truth and enabling me to write this book, which shall become a best seller.

I'm happily married to my wife Paula for the past thirty-two years. She's not only my wife but my lover and my king. Jesus is King of kings. Together, we are the proud parents of four handsome sons: Peter A., Paul A., Phillip A., and Pharez A. Hamilton. We are the grandparents of four children: Phillip Junior, Rociaa (the first princess in the family), Philine, and Invioaa (better known as Army).

I thank God for my beautiful and wonderful family, for their love, support and prayers in writing and putting this book together.

I'm also the author of *Discovering Your Purpose*. I am the senior pastor of Word of Reconciliation International Ministry Inc. located in Albany, New York. This is a no-nonsense ministry where Jesus Christ is Lord.

For more information, email pastorpeter35@gmail.com.

Thank You, Jesus

Printed in the United States
by Baker & Taylor Publisher Services